Oral History: A Very Short Introduction

VERY SHORT INTRODUCTIONS are for anyone wanting a stimulating and accessible way into a new subject. They are written by experts, and have been translated into more than 45 different languages.

The series began in 1995, and now covers a wide variety of topics in every discipline. The VSI library currently contains over 750 volumes—a Very Short Introduction to everything from Psychology and Philosophy of Science to American History and Relativity—and continues to grow in every subject area.

Very Short Introductions available now:

ABOLITIONISM Richard S. Newman
THE ABRAHAMIC RELIGIONS
   Charles L. Cohen
ACCOUNTING Christopher Nobes
ADDICTION Keith Humphreys
ADOLESCENCE Peter K. Smith
THEODOR W. ADORNO
   Andrew Bowie
ADVERTISING Winston Fletcher
AERIAL WARFARE Frank Ledwidge
AESTHETICS Bence Nanay
AFRICAN AMERICAN HISTORY
   Jonathan Scott Holloway
AFRICAN AMERICAN RELIGION
   Eddie S. Glaude Jr.
AFRICAN HISTORY John Parker and
   Richard Rathbone
AFRICAN POLITICS Ian Taylor
AFRICAN RELIGIONS
   Jacob K. Olupona
AGATHA CHRISTIE Gill Plain
AGEING Nancy A. Pachana
AGNOSTICISM Robin Le Poidevin
AGRICULTURE Paul Brassley and
   Richard Soffe
ALEXANDER THE GREAT
   Hugh Bowden
ALGEBRA Peter M. Higgins
AMERICAN BUSINESS HISTORY
   Walter A. Friedman
AMERICAN CULTURAL HISTORY
   Eric Avila
AMERICAN FOREIGN RELATIONS
   Andrew Preston

AMERICAN HISTORY Paul S. Boyer
AMERICAN IMMIGRATION
   David A. Gerber
AMERICAN INTELLECTUAL HISTORY
   Jennifer Ratner-Rosenhagen
THE AMERICAN JUDICIAL SYSTEM
   Charles L. Zelden
AMERICAN LEGAL HISTORY
   G. Edward White
AMERICAN MILITARY HISTORY
   Joseph T. Glatthaar
AMERICAN NAVAL HISTORY
   Craig L. Symonds
AMERICAN POETRY David Caplan
AMERICAN POLITICAL HISTORY
   Donald Critchlow
AMERICAN POLITICAL PARTIES
   AND ELECTIONS L. Sandy Maisel
AMERICAN POLITICS
   Richard M. Valelly
THE AMERICAN PRESIDENCY
   Charles O. Jones
THE AMERICAN REVOLUTION
   Robert J. Allison
AMERICAN SLAVERY
   Heather Andrea Williams
THE AMERICAN SOUTH
   Charles Reagan Wilson
THE AMERICAN WEST
   Stephen Aron
AMERICAN WOMEN'S HISTORY
   Susan Ware
AMPHIBIANS T. S. Kemp
ANAESTHESIA Aidan O'Donnell

- ANALYTIC PHILOSOPHY Michael Beaney
- ANARCHISM Alex Prichard
- ANCIENT ASSYRIA Karen Radner
- ANCIENT EGYPT Ian Shaw
- ANCIENT EGYPTIAN ART AND ARCHITECTURE Christina Riggs
- ANCIENT GREECE Paul Cartledge
- ANCIENT GREEK AND ROMAN SCIENCE Liba Taub
- THE ANCIENT NEAR EAST Amanda H. Podany
- ANCIENT PHILOSOPHY Julia Annas
- ANCIENT WARFARE Harry Sidebottom
- ANGELS David Albert Jones
- ANGLICANISM Mark Chapman
- THE ANGLO-SAXON AGE John Blair
- ANIMAL BEHAVIOUR Tristram D. Wyatt
- THE ANIMAL KINGDOM Peter Holland
- ANIMAL RIGHTS David DeGrazia
- ANSELM Thomas Williams
- THE ANTARCTIC Klaus Dodds
- ANTHROPOCENE Erle C. Ellis
- ANTISEMITISM Steven Beller
- ANXIETY Daniel Freeman and Jason Freeman
- THE APOCRYPHAL GOSPELS Paul Foster
- APPLIED MATHEMATICS Alain Goriely
- THOMAS AQUINAS Fergus Kerr
- ARBITRATION Thomas Schultz and Thomas Grant
- ARCHAEOLOGY Paul Bahn
- ARCHITECTURE Andrew Ballantyne
- THE ARCTIC Klaus Dodds and Jamie Woodward
- HANNAH ARENDT Dana Villa
- ARISTOCRACY William Doyle
- ARISTOTLE Jonathan Barnes
- ART HISTORY Dana Arnold
- ART THEORY Cynthia Freeland
- ARTIFICIAL INTELLIGENCE Margaret A. Boden
- ASIAN AMERICAN HISTORY Madeline Y. Hsu
- ASTROBIOLOGY David C. Catling
- ASTROPHYSICS James Binney
- ATHEISM Julian Baggini
- THE ATMOSPHERE Paul I. Palmer
- AUGUSTINE Henry Chadwick
- JANE AUSTEN Tom Keymer
- AUSTRALIA Kenneth Morgan
- AUTHORITARIANISM James Loxton
- AUTISM Uta Frith
- AUTOBIOGRAPHY Laura Marcus
- THE AVANT GARDE David Cottington
- THE AZTECS Davíd Carrasco
- BABYLONIA Trevor Bryce
- BACTERIA Sebastian G. B. Amyes
- BANKING John Goddard and John O. S. Wilson
- BARTHES Jonathan Culler
- THE BEATS David Sterritt
- BEAUTY Roger Scruton
- LUDWIG VAN BEETHOVEN Mark Evan Bonds
- BEHAVIOURAL ECONOMICS Michelle Baddeley
- BESTSELLERS John Sutherland
- THE BIBLE John Riches
- BIBLICAL ARCHAEOLOGY Eric H. Cline
- BIG DATA Dawn E. Holmes
- BIOCHEMISTRY Mark Lorch
- BIODIVERSITY CONSERVATION David Macdonald
- BIOGEOGRAPHY Mark V. Lomolino
- BIOGRAPHY Hermione Lee
- BIOMETRICS Michael Fairhurst
- ELIZABETH BISHOP Jonathan F. S. Post
- BLACK HOLES Katherine Blundell
- BLASPHEMY Yvonne Sherwood
- BLOOD Chris Cooper
- THE BLUES Elijah Wald
- THE BODY Chris Shilling
- THE BOHEMIANS David Weir
- NIELS BOHR J. L. Heilbron
- THE BOOK OF COMMON PRAYER Brian Cummings
- THE BOOK OF MORMON Terryl Givens
- BORDERS Alexander C. Diener and Joshua Hagen
- JORGE LUIS BORGES Ilan Stavans
- THE BRAIN Michael O'Shea

BRANDING Robert Jones
THE BRICS Andrew F. Cooper
BRITISH ARCHITECTURE
    Dana Arnold
BRITISH CINEMA Charles Barr
THE BRITISH CONSTITUTION
    Martin Loughlin
THE BRITISH EMPIRE Ashley Jackson
BRITISH POLITICS Tony Wright
BUDDHA Michael Carrithers
BUDDHISM Damien Keown
BUDDHIST ETHICS Damien Keown
BYZANTIUM Peter Sarris
CALVINISM Jon Balserak
ALBERT CAMUS Oliver Gloag
CANADA Donald Wright
CANCER Nicholas James
CAPITALISM James Fulcher
CATHOLICISM Gerald O'Collins
THE CATHOLIC REFORMATION
    James E. Kelly
CAUSATION Stephen Mumford and
    Rani Lill Anjum
THE CELL Terence Allen and
    Graham Cowling
THE CELTS Barry Cunliffe
CHAOS Leonard Smith
GEOFFREY CHAUCER David Wallace
CHEMISTRY Peter Atkins
CHILD PSYCHOLOGY Usha Goswami
CHILDREN'S LITERATURE
    Kimberley Reynolds
CHINESE LITERATURE Sabina Knight
CHOICE THEORY Michael Allingham
CHRISTIAN ART Beth Williamson
CHRISTIAN ETHICS D. Stephen Long
CHRISTIANITY Linda Woodhead
CICERO Yelena Baraz
CIRCADIAN RHYTHMS
    Russell Foster and Leon Kreitzman
CITIZENSHIP Richard Bellamy
CITY PLANNING Carl Abbott
CIVIL ENGINEERING
    David Muir Wood
THE CIVIL RIGHTS MOVEMENT
    Thomas C. Holt
CIVIL WARS Monica Duffy Toft
CLASSICAL LITERATURE William Allan
CLASSICAL MYTHOLOGY
    Helen Morales
CLASSICS Mary Beard and
    John Henderson
CLAUSEWITZ Michael Howard
CLIMATE Mark Maslin
CLIMATE CHANGE Mark Maslin
CLINICAL PSYCHOLOGY Susan Llewelyn
    and Katie Aafjes-van Doorn
COGNITIVE BEHAVIOURAL
    THERAPY Freda McManus
COGNITIVE NEUROSCIENCE
    Richard Passingham
THE COLD WAR Robert J. McMahon
COLONIAL AMERICA Alan Taylor
COLONIAL LATIN AMERICAN
    LITERATURE Rolena Adorno
COMBINATORICS Robin Wilson
COMEDY Matthew Bevis
COMMUNISM Leslie Holmes
COMPARATIVE LAW Sabrina Ragone
    and Guido Smorto
COMPARATIVE LITERATURE
    Ben Hutchinson
COMPETITION AND ANTITRUST
    LAW Ariel Ezrachi
COMPLEXITY John H. Holland
THE COMPUTER Darrel Ince
COMPUTER SCIENCE
    Subrata Dasgupta
CONCENTRATION CAMPS
    Dan Stone
CONDENSED MATTER PHYSICS
    Ross H. McKenzie
CONFUCIANISM Daniel K. Gardner
THE CONQUISTADORS
    Matthew Restall and
    Felipe Fernández-Armesto
CONSCIENCE Paul Strohm
CONSCIOUSNESS Susan Blackmore
CONTEMPORARY ART
    Julian Stallabrass
CONTEMPORARY FICTION
    Robert Eaglestone
CONTINENTAL PHILOSOPHY
    Simon Critchley
COPERNICUS Owen Gingerich
CORAL REEFS Charles Sheppard
CORPORATE SOCIAL
    RESPONSIBILITY Jeremy Moon
CORRUPTION Leslie Holmes
COSMOLOGY Peter Coles

COUNTRY MUSIC Richard Carlin
CREATIVITY Vlad Glăveanu
CRIME FICTION Richard Bradford
CRIMINAL JUSTICE Julian V. Roberts
CRIMINOLOGY Tim Newburn
CRITICAL THEORY
    Stephen Eric Bronner
THE CRUSADES Christopher Tyerman
CRYPTOGRAPHY Sean Murphy and
    Rachel Player
CRYSTALLOGRAPHY A. M. Glazer
THE CULTURAL REVOLUTION
    Richard Curt Kraus
DADA AND SURREALISM
    David Hopkins
DANTE Peter Hainsworth and
    David Robey
DARWIN Jonathan Howard
THE DEAD SEA SCROLLS
    Timothy H. Lim
DECADENCE David Weir
DECOLONIZATION Dane Kennedy
DEMENTIA Kathleen Taylor
DEMOCRACY Naomi Zack
DEMOGRAPHY Sarah Harper
DEPRESSION Jan Scott and
    Mary Jane Tacchi
DERRIDA Simon Glendinning
DESCARTES Tom Sorell
DESERTS Nick Middleton
DESIGN John Heskett
DEVELOPMENT Ian Goldin
DEVELOPMENTAL BIOLOGY
    Lewis Wolpert
THE DEVIL Darren Oldridge
DIASPORA Kevin Kenny
CHARLES DICKENS Jenny Hartley
DICTIONARIES Lynda Mugglestone
DINOSAURS David Norman
DIPLOMATIC HISTORY
    Joseph M. Siracusa
DOCUMENTARY FILM
    Patricia Aufderheide
DOSTOEVSKY Deborah Martinsen
DREAMING J. Allan Hobson
DRUGS Les Iversen
DRUIDS Barry Cunliffe
DYNASTY Jeroen Duindam
DYSLEXIA Margaret J. Snowling
EARLY MUSIC Thomas Forrest Kelly
THE EARTH Martin Redfern
EARTH SYSTEM SCIENCE Tim Lenton
ECOLOGY Jaboury Ghazoul
ECONOMICS Partha Dasgupta
EDUCATION Gary Thomas
EGYPTIAN MYTH Geraldine Pinch
EIGHTEENTH-CENTURY BRITAIN
    Paul Langford
ELECTIONS L. Sandy Maisel and
    Jennifer A. Yoder
THE ELEMENTS Philip Ball
GEORGE ELIOT Juliette Atkinson
EMOTION Dylan Evans
EMPIRE Stephen Howe
EMPLOYMENT LAW David Cabrelli
ENERGY SYSTEMS Nick Jenkins
ENGELS Terrell Carver
ENGINEERING David Blockley
THE ENGLISH LANGUAGE
    Simon Horobin
ENGLISH LITERATURE
    Jonathan Bate
THE ENLIGHTENMENT
    John Robertson
ENTREPRENEURSHIP Paul Westhead
    and Mike Wright
ENTROPY James Binney
ENVIRONMENTAL ECONOMICS
    Stephen Smith
ENVIRONMENTAL ETHICS
    Robin Attfield
ENVIRONMENTAL LAW
    Elizabeth Fisher
ENVIRONMENTAL POLITICS
    Andrew Dobson
ENZYMES Paul Engel
THE EPIC Anthony Welch
EPICUREANISM Catherine Wilson
EPIDEMIOLOGY Rodolfo Saracci
ETHICS Simon Blackburn
ETHNOMUSICOLOGY Timothy Rice
THE ETRUSCANS Christopher Smith
EUGENICS Philippa Levine
THE EUROPEAN UNION
    Simon Usherwood and John Pinder
EUROPEAN UNION LAW
    Anthony Arnull
EVANGELICALISM
    John G. Stackhouse Jr.
EVIL Luke Russell

EVOLUTION Brian and
    Deborah Charlesworth
EXISTENTIALISM Thomas Flynn
EXPLORATION Stewart A. Weaver
EXTINCTION Paul B. Wignall
THE EYE Michael Land
FAIRY TALE Marina Warner
FAITH Roger Trigg
FAMILY LAW Jonathan Herring
MICHAEL FARADAY
    Frank A. J. L. James
FASCISM Kevin Passmore
FASHION Rebecca Arnold
FEDERALISM Mark J. Rozell and
    Clyde Wilcox
FEMINISM Margaret Walters
FEMINIST PHILOSOPHY
    Katharine Jenkins
FILM Michael Wood
FILM MUSIC Kathryn Kalinak
FILM NOIR James Naremore
FIRE Andrew C. Scott
THE FIRST WORLD WAR
    Michael Howard
FLUID MECHANICS Eric Lauga
FOLK MUSIC Mark Slobin
FOOD John Krebs
FORENSIC PSYCHOLOGY
    David Canter
FORENSIC SCIENCE Jim Fraser
FORESTS Jaboury Ghazoul
FOSSILS Keith Thomson
FOUCAULT Gary Gutting
THE FOUNDING FATHERS
    R. B. Bernstein
FRACTALS Kenneth Falconer
FREE SPEECH Nigel Warburton
FREE WILL Thomas Pink
FREEMASONRY Andreas Önnerfors
FRENCH CINEMA Dudley Andrew
FRENCH LITERATURE John D. Lyons
FRENCH PHILOSOPHY
    Stephen Gaukroger and Knox Peden
THE FRENCH REVOLUTION
    William Doyle
FREUD Anthony Storr
FUNDAMENTALISM Malise Ruthven
FUNGI Nicholas P. Money
THE FUTURE Jennifer M. Gidley
FUTURSM Ara Merjian
GALAXIES John Gribbin
GALILEO Stillman Drake
GAME THEORY Ken Binmore
GANDHI Bhikhu Parekh
GARDEN HISTORY Gordon Campbell
GENDER HISTORY Antoinette Burton
GENES Jonathan Slack
GENIUS Andrew Robinson
GENOMICS John Archibald
GEOGRAPHY John Matthews and
    David Herbert
GEOLOGY Jan Zalasiewicz
GEOMETRY Maciej Dunajski
GEOPHYSICAL AND CLIMATE
    HAZARDS Bill McGuire
GEOPHYSICS William Lowrie
GEOPOLITICS Klaus Dodds
GERMAN LITERATURE Nicholas Boyle
GERMAN PHILOSOPHY
    Andrew Bowie
THE GHETTO Bryan Cheyette
GLACIATION David J. A. Evans
GLOBAL ECONOMIC HISTORY
    Robert C. Allen
GLOBAL ISLAM Nile Green
GLOBALIZATION Manfred B. Steger
GOD John Bowker
GÖDEL'S THEOREM A. W. Moore
GOETHE Ritchie Robertson
THE GOTHIC Nick Groom
GOVERNANCE Mark Bevir
GRAVITY Timothy Clifton
THE GREAT DEPRESSION AND THE
    NEW DEAL Eric Rauchway
THE GULAG Alan Barenberg
HABEAS CORPUS Amanda L. Tyler
HABERMAS James Gordon Finlayson
THE HABSBURG EMPIRE
    Martyn Rady
HAPPINESS Daniel M. Haybron
THE HARLEM RENAISSANCE
    Cheryl A. Wall
THE HEBREW BIBLE AS
    LITERATURE Tod Linafelt
HEGEL Peter Singer
HEIDEGGER Michael Inwood
THE HELLENISTIC AGE
    Peter Thonemann
HEREDITY John Waller
HERMENEUTICS Jens Zimmermann

HERODOTUS Jennifer T. Roberts
HIEROGLYPHS Penelope Wilson
HINDUISM Kim Knott
HISTORY John H. Arnold
THE HISTORY OF ASTRONOMY
    Michael Hoskin
THE HISTORY OF CHEMISTRY
    William H. Brock
THE HISTORY OF CHILDHOOD
    James Marten
THE HISTORY OF CINEMA
    Geoffrey Nowell-Smith
THE HISTORY OF COMPUTING
    Doron Swade
THE HISTORY OF EMOTIONS
    Thomas Dixon
THE HISTORY OF LIFE Michael Benton
THE HISTORY OF MATHEMATICS
    Jacqueline Stedall
THE HISTORY OF MEDICINE
    William Bynum
THE HISTORY OF PHYSICS
    J. L. Heilbron
THE HISTORY OF POLITICAL
    THOUGHT Richard Whatmore
THE HISTORY OF TIME
    Leofranc Holford-Strevens
HIV AND AIDS Alan Whiteside
HOBBES Richard Tuck
HOLLYWOOD Peter Decherney
THE HOLY ROMAN EMPIRE
    Joachim Whaley
HOME Michael Allen Fox
HOMER Barbara Graziosi
HORACE Llewelyn Morgan
HORMONES Martin Luck
HORROR Darryl Jones
HUMAN ANATOMY Leslie Klenerman
HUMAN EVOLUTION
    Bernard Wood
HUMAN GEOGRAPHY Patricia Daley
    and Ian Klinke
HUMAN PHYSIOLOGY
    Jamie A. Davies
HUMAN RESOURCE MANAGEMENT
    Adrian Wilkinson
HUMAN RIGHTS Andrew Clapham
HUMANISM Stephen Law
HUME James A. Harris
HUMOUR Noël Carroll

IBN SĪNĀ (AVICENNA)
    Peter Adamson
THE ICE AGE Jamie Woodward
IDENTITY Florian Coulmas
IDEOLOGY Michael Freeden
IMAGINATION
    Jennifer Gosetti-Ferencei
THE IMMUNE SYSTEM
    Paul Klenerman
INDIAN CINEMA
    Ashish Rajadhyaksha
INDIAN PHILOSOPHY Sue Hamilton
THE INDUSTRIAL REVOLUTION
    Robert C. Allen
INFECTIOUS DISEASE Marta L. Wayne
    and Benjamin M. Bolker
INFINITY Ian Stewart
INFORMATION Luciano Floridi
INNOVATION Mark Dodgson and
    David Gann
INSECTS Simon Leather
INTELLECTUAL PROPERTY
    Siva Vaidhyanathan
INTELLIGENCE Ian J. Deary
INTERNATIONAL LAW
    Vaughan Lowe
INTERNATIONAL MIGRATION
    Khalid Koser
INTERNATIONAL RELATIONS
    Christian Reus-Smit
INTERNATIONAL SECURITY
    Christopher S. Browning
INVASIVE SPECIES Julie Lockwood and
    Dustin Welbourne
IRAN Ali M. Ansari
ISLAM Malise Ruthven
ISLAMIC HISTORY Adam Silverstein
ISLAMIC LAW Mashood A. Baderin
ISOTOPES Rob Ellam
ITALIAN LITERATURE
    Peter Hainsworth and David Robey
HENRY JAMES Susan L. Mizruchi
JAPANESE LITERATURE Alan Tansman
JESUS Richard Bauckham
JEWISH HISTORY David N. Myers
JEWISH LITERATURE Ilan Stavans
JOURNALISM Ian Hargreaves
JAMES JOYCE Colin MacCabe
JUDAISM Norman Solomon
JUNG Anthony Stevens

THE JURY Renée Lettow Lerner
KABBALAH Joseph Dan
KAFKA Ritchie Robertson
KANT Roger Scruton
KEYNES Robert Skidelsky
KIERKEGAARD Patrick Gardiner
KNOWLEDGE Jennifer Nagel
THE KORAN Michael Cook
KOREA Michael J. Seth
LAKES Warwick F. Vincent
LANDSCAPE ARCHITECTURE
    Ian H. Thompson
LANDSCAPES AND
    GEOMORPHOLOGY
    Andrew Goudie and Heather Viles
LANGUAGES Stephen R. Anderson
LATE ANTIQUITY Gillian Clark
LAW Raymond Wacks
THE LAWS OF THERMODYNAMICS
    Peter Atkins
LEADERSHIP Keith Grint
LEARNING Mark Haselgrove
LEIBNIZ Maria Rosa Antognazza
C. S. LEWIS James Como
LIBERALISM Michael Freeden
LIGHT Ian Walmsley
LINCOLN Allen C. Guelzo
LINGUISTICS Peter Matthews
LITERARY THEORY Jonathan Culler
LOCKE John Dunn
LOGIC Graham Priest
LOVE Ronald de Sousa
MARTIN LUTHER Scott H. Hendrix
MACHIAVELLI Quentin Skinner
MADNESS Andrew Scull
MAGIC Owen Davies
MAGNA CARTA Nicholas Vincent
MAGNETISM Stephen Blundell
MOSES MAIMONIDES Ross Brann
MALTHUS Donald Winch
MAMMALS T. S. Kemp
MANAGEMENT John Hendry
NELSON MANDELA Elleke Boehmer
MAO Delia Davin
MARINE BIOLOGY Philip V. Mladenov
MARKETING
    Kenneth Le Meunier-FitzHugh
THE MARQUIS DE SADE John Phillips
MARTYRDOM Jolyon Mitchell
MARX Peter Singer

MATERIALS Christopher Hall
MATHEMATICAL ANALYSIS
    Richard Earl
MATHEMATICAL FINANCE
    Mark H. A. Davis
MATHEMATICS Timothy Gowers
MATTER Geoff Cottrell
THE MAYA Matthew Restall and
    Amara Solari
MEANING Emma Borg and
    Sarah A. Fisher
THE MEANING OF LIFE
    Terry Eagleton
MEASUREMENT David Hand
MEDICAL ETHICS Michael Dunn and
    Tony Hope
MEDICAL LAW Charles Foster
MEDIEVAL BRITAIN John Gillingham
    and Ralph A. Griffiths
MEDIEVAL LITERATURE
    Elaine Treharne
MEDIEVAL PHILOSOPHY
    John Marenbon
MEMORY Jonathan K. Foster
METAPHYSICS Stephen Mumford
METHODISM William J. Abraham
THE MEXICAN REVOLUTION
    Alan Knight
MICROBIOLOGY Nicholas P. Money
MICROBIOMES Angela E. Douglas
MICROECONOMICS Avinash Dixit
MICROSCOPY Terence Allen
THE MIDDLE AGES Miri Rubin
MILITARY JUSTICE Eugene R. Fidell
MILITARY STRATEGY
    Antulio J. Echevarria II
JOHN STUART MILL Gregory Claeys
MINERALS David Vaughan
MIRACLES Yujin Nagasawa
MODERN ARCHITECTURE
    Adam Sharr
MODERN ART David Cottington
MODERN BRAZIL Anthony W. Pereira
MODERN CHINA Rana Mitter
MODERN DRAMA
    Kirsten E. Shepherd-Barr
MODERN FRANCE
    Vanessa R. Schwartz
MODERN INDIA Craig Jeffrey
MODERN IRELAND Senia Pašeta

MODERN ITALY Anna Cento Bull
MODERN JAPAN
    Christopher Goto-Jones
MODERN LATIN AMERICAN
    LITERATURE
    Roberto González Echevarría
MODERN WAR Richard English
MODERNISM Christopher Butler
MOLECULAR BIOLOGY Aysha Divan
    and Janice A. Royds
MOLECULES Philip Ball
MONASTICISM Stephen J. Davis
THE MONGOLS Morris Rossabi
MONTAIGNE William M. Hamlin
MOONS David A. Rothery
MORMONISM Richard Lyman Bushman
MOUNTAINS Martin F. Price
MUHAMMAD Jonathan A. C. Brown
MULTICULTURALISM Ali Rattansi
MULTILINGUALISM John C. Maher
MUSIC Nicholas Cook
MUSIC AND TECHNOLOGY
    Mark Katz
MYTH Robert A. Segal
NANOTECHNOLOGY
    Philip Moriarty
NAPOLEON David A. Bell
THE NAPOLEONIC WARS
    Mike Rapport
NATIONALISM Steven Grosby
NATIVE AMERICAN LITERATURE
    Sean Teuton
NAVIGATION Jim Bennett
NAZI GERMANY Jane Caplan
NEGOTIATION Carrie Menkel-Meadow
NEOLIBERALISM Manfred B. Steger
    and Ravi K. Roy
NETWORKS Guido Caldarelli and
    Michele Catanzaro
THE NEW TESTAMENT
    Luke Timothy Johnson
THE NEW TESTAMENT AS
    LITERATURE Kyle Keefer
NEWTON Robert Iliffe
NIETZSCHE Michael Tanner
NINETEENTH-CENTURY BRITAIN
    Christopher Harvie and
    H. C. G. Matthew
THE NORMAN CONQUEST
    George Garnett

NORTH AMERICAN INDIANS
    Theda Perdue and Michael D. Green
NORTHERN IRELAND
    Marc Mulholland
NOTHING Frank Close
NUCLEAR PHYSICS Frank Close
NUCLEAR POWER Maxwell Irvine
NUCLEAR WEAPONS
    Joseph M. Siracusa
NUMBER THEORY Robin Wilson
NUMBERS Peter M. Higgins
NUTRITION David A. Bender
OBJECTIVITY Stephen Gaukroger
OBSERVATIONAL ASTRONOMY
    Geoff Cottrell
OCEANS Dorrik Stow
THE OLD TESTAMENT
    Michael D. Coogan
ORAL HISTORY Douglas A. Boyd
THE ORCHESTRA D. Kern Holoman
ORGANIC CHEMISTRY
    Graham Patrick
ORGANIZATIONS Mary Jo Hatch
ORGANIZED CRIME
    Georgios A. Antonopoulos and
    Georgios Papanicolaou
ORTHODOX CHRISTIANITY
    A. Edward Siecienski
OVID Llewelyn Morgan
PAGANISM Owen Davies
PAKISTAN Pippa Virdee
THE PALESTINIAN-ISRAELI
    CONFLICT Martin Bunton
PANDEMICS Christian W. McMillen
PARTICLE PHYSICS Frank Close
PAUL E. P. Sanders
IVAN PAVLOV Daniel P. Todes
PEACE Oliver P. Richmond
PENTECOSTALISM William K. Kay
PERCEPTION Brian Rogers
THE PERIODIC TABLE Eric R. Scerri
PHILOSOPHICAL METHOD
    Timothy Williamson
PHILOSOPHY Edward Craig
PHILOSOPHY IN THE ISLAMIC
    WORLD Peter Adamson
PHILOSOPHY OF BIOLOGY
    Samir Okasha
PHILOSOPHY OF LAW
    Raymond Wacks

PHILOSOPHY OF MIND Barbara Gail Montero
PHILOSOPHY OF PHYSICS David Wallace
PHILOSOPHY OF SCIENCE Samir Okasha
PHILOSOPHY OF RELIGION Tim Bayne
PHOTOGRAPHY Steve Edwards
PHYSICAL CHEMISTRY Peter Atkins
PHYSICS Sidney Perkowitz
PILGRIMAGE Ian Reader
PLAGUE Paul Slack
PLANETARY SYSTEMS Raymond T. Pierrehumbert
PLANETS David A. Rothery
PLANTS Timothy Walker
PLATE TECTONICS Peter Molnar
SYLVIA PLATH Heather Clark
PLATO Julia Annas
POETRY Bernard O'Donoghue
POLITICAL PHILOSOPHY David Miller
POLITICS Kenneth Minogue
POLYGAMY Sarah M. S. Pearsall
POPULISM Cas Mudde and Cristóbal Rovira Kaltwasser
POSTCOLONIALISM Robert J. C. Young
POSTMODERNISM Christopher Butler
POSTSTRUCTURALISM Catherine Belsey
POSTWAR EUROPE Richard Bessel
POVERTY Philip N. Jefferson
PREHISTORY Chris Gosden
PRESOCRATIC PHILOSOPHY Catherine Osborne
PRIVACY Raymond Wacks
PROBABILITY John Haigh
PROGRESSIVISM Walter Nugent
PROHIBITION W. J. Rorabaugh
PROJECTS Andrew Davies
PROTESTANTISM Mark A. Noll
MARCEL PROUST Joshua Landy
PSEUDOSCIENCE Michael D. Gordin
PSYCHIATRY Tom Burns
PSYCHOANALYSIS Daniel Pick
PSYCHOLINGUISTICS Ferenda Ferreria
PSYCHOLOGY Gillian Butler and Freda McManus
PSYCHOLOGY OF MUSIC Elizabeth Hellmuth Margulis
PSYCHOPATHY Essi Viding
PSYCHOTHERAPY Tom Burns and Eva Burns-Lundgren
PUBLIC ADMINISTRATION Stella Z. Theodoulou and Ravi K. Roy
PUBLIC HEALTH Virginia Berridge
PURITANISM Francis J. Bremer
THE QUAKERS Pink Dandelion
QUANTUM THEORY John Polkinghorne
RACISM Ali Rattansi
RADIOACTIVITY Claudio Tuniz
RASTAFARI Ennis B. Edmonds
READING Belinda Jack
THE REAGAN REVOLUTION Gil Troy
REALITY Jan Westerhoff
RECONSTRUCTION Allen C. Guelzo
THE REFORMATION Peter Marshall
REFUGEES Gil Loescher
RELATIVITY Russell Stannard
RELIGION Thomas A. Tweed
RELIGION IN AMERICA Timothy Beal
THE RENAISSANCE Jerry Brotton
RENAISSANCE ART Geraldine A. Johnson
RENEWABLE ENERGY Nick Jelley
REPTILES T. S. Kemp
REVOLUTIONS Jack A. Goldstone
RHETORIC Richard Toye
RISK Baruch Fischhoff and John Kadvany
RITUAL Barry Stephenson
RIVERS Nick Middleton
ROBOTICS Alan Winfield
ROCKS Jan Zalasiewicz
ROMAN BRITAIN Peter Salway
THE ROMAN EMPIRE Christopher Kelly
THE ROMAN REPUBLIC David M. Gwynn
ROMANTICISM Michael Ferber
ROUSSEAU Robert Wokler
THE RULE OF LAW Aziz Z. Huq
RUSSELL A. C. Grayling
THE RUSSIAN ECONOMY Richard Connolly
RUSSIAN HISTORY Geoffrey Hosking
RUSSIAN LITERATURE Catriona Kelly
RUSSIAN POLITICS Brian D. Taylor

THE RUSSIAN REVOLUTION
  S. A. Smith
SAINTS Simon Yarrow
SAMURAI Michael Wert
SAVANNAS Peter A. Furley
SCEPTICISM Duncan Pritchard
SCHIZOPHRENIA Chris Frith and
  Eve Johnstone
SCHOPENHAUER
  Christopher Janaway
SCIENCE AND RELIGION
  Thomas Dixon and Adam R. Shapiro
SCIENCE FICTION David Seed
THE SCIENTIFIC REVOLUTION
  Lawrence M. Principe
SCOTLAND Rab Houston
SECULARISM Andrew Copson
THE SELF Marya Schechtman
SEXUAL SELECTION Marlene Zuk and
  Leigh W. Simmons
SEXUALITY Véronique Mottier
WILLIAM SHAKESPEARE
  Stanley Wells
SHAKESPEARE'S COMEDIES
  Bart van Es
SHAKESPEARE'S SONNETS AND
  POEMS Jonathan F. S. Post
SHAKESPEARE'S TRAGEDIES
  Stanley Wells
GEORGE BERNARD SHAW
  Christopher Wixson
MARY SHELLEY Charlotte Gordon
THE SHORT STORY Andrew Kahn
SIKHISM Eleanor Nesbitt
SILENT FILM Donna Kornhaber
THE SILK ROAD James A. Millward
SLANG Jonathon Green
SLEEP Steven W. Lockley and
  Russell G. Foster
SMELL Matthew Cobb
ADAM SMITH Christopher J. Berry
SOCIAL AND CULTURAL
  ANTHROPOLOGY
  John Monaghan and Peter Just
SOCIALISM Michael Newman
SOCIAL PSYCHOLOGY Richard J. Crisp
SOCIAL SCIENCE Alexander Betts
SOCIAL WORK Sally Holland and
  Jonathan Scourfield
SOCIOLINGUISTICS John Edwards
SOCIOLOGY Steve Bruce
SOCRATES C. C. W. Taylor
SOFT MATTER Tom McLeish
SOPHOCLES Edith Hall
SOUND Mike Goldsmith
SOUTHEAST ASIA James R. Rush
THE SOVIET UNION Stephen Lovell
THE SPANISH CIVIL WAR
  Helen Graham
SPANISH LITERATURE Jo Labanyi
THE SPARTANS Andrew J. Bayliss
SPINOZA Roger Scruton
SPIRITUALITY Philip Sheldrake
SPORT Mike Cronin
STARS Andrew King
STATISTICS David J. Hand
STEM CELLS Jonathan Slack
STOICISM Brad Inwood
STRUCTURAL ENGINEERING
  David Blockley
STUART BRITAIN John Morrill
SUBURBS Carl Abbott
THE SUN Philip Judge
SUPERCONDUCTIVITY
  Stephen Blundell
SUPERSTITION Stuart Vyse
SURVEILLANCE David Lyon
SUSTAINABILITY Saleem Ali
SYMBIOSIS Nancy A. Moran
SYMMETRY Ian Stewart
SYNAESTHESIA Julia Simner
SYNTHETIC BIOLOGY Jamie A. Davies
SYSTEMS BIOLOGY Eberhard O. Voit
TAXATION Stephen Smith
TEETH Peter S. Ungar
TERRORISM Charles Townshend
THEATRE Marvin Carlson
THEOLOGY David F. Ford
THINKING AND REASONING
  Jonathan St B. T. Evans
HENRY DAVID THOREAU
  Lawrence Buell
THOUGHT Tim Bayne
THUCYDIDES Jennifer T. Roberts
TIBETAN BUDDHISM
  Matthew T. Kapstein
TIDES David George Bowers and
  Emyr Martyn Roberts
TIME Jenann Ismael
TOCQUEVILLE Harvey C. Mansfield

TOLERATION Andrew Murphy
J. R. R. TOLKIEN Matthew Townend
LEO TOLSTOY Liza Knapp
TOPOLOGY Richard Earl
TRAGEDY Adrian Poole
TRANSLATION Matthew Reynolds
THE TREATY OF VERSAILLES
    Michael S. Neiberg
TRIGONOMETRY
    Glen Van Brummelen
THE TROJAN WAR Eric H. Cline
ANTHONY TROLLOPE Dinah Birch
TRUST Katherine Hawley
THE TUDORS John Guy
TWENTIETH-CENTURY BRITAIN
    Kenneth O. Morgan
TYPOGRAPHY Paul Luna
THE UNITED NATIONS
    Jussi M. Hanhimäki
UNIVERSITIES AND COLLEGES
    David Palfreyman and Paul Temple
THE U.S. CIVIL WAR Louis P. Masur
THE U.S. CONGRESS Donald A. Ritchie
THE U.S. CONSTITUTION
    David J. Bodenhamer
THE U.S. SUPREME COURT
    Linda Greenhouse
UTILITARIANISM
    Katarzyna de Lazari-Radek and
    Peter Singer
UTOPIANISM Lyman Tower Sargent
VATICAN II Shaun Blanchard and
    Stephen Bullivant

VETERINARY SCIENCE James Yeates
THE VICTORIANS Martin Hewitt
THE VIKINGS Julian D. Richards
VIOLENCE Philip Dwyer
THE VIRGIN MARY
    Mary Joan Winn Leith
THE VIRTUES Craig A. Boyd and
    Kevin Timpe
VIRUSES Dorothy H. Crawford
VOLCANOES Michael J. Branney and
    Jan Zalasiewicz
VOLTAIRE Nicholas Cronk
WAR AND RELIGION Jolyon Mitchell
    and Joshua Rey
WAR AND TECHNOLOGY
    Alex Roland
WATER John Finney
WAVES Mike Goldsmith
WEATHER Storm Dunlop
SIMONE WEIL A. Rebecca Rozelle-Stone
THE WELFARE STATE David Garland
WITCHCRAFT Malcolm Gaskill
WITTGENSTEIN A. C. Grayling
WORK Stephen Fineman
WORLD MUSIC Philip Bohlman
WORLD MYTHOLOGY David Leeming
THE WORLD TRADE
    ORGANIZATION Amrita Narlikar
WORLD WAR II Gerhard L. Weinberg
WRITING AND SCRIPT
    Andrew Robinson
ZIONISM Michael Stanislawski
ÉMILE ZOLA Brian Nelson

Available soon:

ADMINISTRATIVE LAW
    Stephen Thomson

EVOLUTIONARY PSYCHOLOGY
    Maryanne Fisher and T. Joel Wade
HERMAN MELVILLE Maurice S. Lee

For more information visit our website

www.oup.com/vsi/

Douglas A. Boyd

ORAL HISTORY

A Very Short Introduction

OXFORD
UNIVERSITY PRESS

Oxford University Press is a department of the University of Oxford.
It furthers the University's objective of excellence in research, scholarship,
and education by publishing worldwide. Oxford is a registered trade mark of
Oxford University Press in the UK and in certain other countries.

Published in the United States of America by Oxford University Press
198 Madison Avenue, New York, NY 10016, United States of America.

© Oxford University Press 2025

All rights reserved. No part of this publication may be reproduced, stored in a retrieval system, transmitted, used for text and data mining, or used for training artificial intelligence, in any form or by any means, without the prior permission in writing of Oxford University Press, or as expressly permitted by law, by license or under terms agreed with the appropriate reprographics rights organization. Inquiries concerning reproduction outside the scope of the above should be sent to the Rights Department, Oxford University Press, at the address above.

You must not circulate this work in any other form
and you must impose this same condition on any acquirer.

CIP data is on file at the Library of Congress.

ISBN 9780190067625

DOI: 10.1093/9780190067632.001.0001

Printed by Integrated Books International, United States of America

The manufacturer's authorized representative in the EU for product safety is
Oxford University Press España S.A. of Parque Empresarial San Fernando de Henares,
Avenida de Castilla, 2 – 28830 Madrid (www.oup.es/en or product.safety@oup.com).
OUP España S.A. also acts as importer into Spain of products made by the manufacturer.

Contents

List of illustrations xvii

Preface xix

1 Tell me a little about yourself 1

2 Defining oral history through time 14

3 Asking questions: The oral history interview 41

4 Designing an oral history project 70

5 The archival impact of oral history 99

References 111

Further reading 119

Index 127

List of illustrations

1. A child interviews a coal miner in Kentucky, c. 1981 **4**
   Kentucky Historical Society, KOHC slide collection

2. John Peabody Harrington, an ethnologist working for the Bureau of American Ethnology, interviews Margarita (Marguerite) Compos, a member of the Guna community, 1924 **28**
   Courtesy of the Library of Congress and the Smithsonian Institution

3. Indira Chowdhury interviews Dipali Pramanik at Kolaghat Mahila Samiti, Kolaghat, West Bengal, for the Sasha Association for Craft Producers, 2015 **49**
   Courtesy of Indira Chowdhury. Photograph by Avehi Menon

4. Tanya Pearson interviews Shirley Manson for the Women of Rock Oral History Project, 2018 **65**
   Courtesy of Tanya Pearson. Project housed at the Sophia Smith Collection at Smith College

5. J. Wells interviews Samara Davis, founder of the Black Bourbon Society, for the Black Women in Bourbon Oral History Project, 2022 **76**
   Courtesy of the Louie B. Nunn Center for Oral History, University of Kentucky Libraries. Photograph by Douglas A. Boyd

6. Recording equipment that was once commonplace in oral history: the Sony TCM 5000ev Cassette-Corder, the Marantz PMD222 Portable Cassette Recorder, and an audio cassette **83**
   Photograph by Douglas A. Boyd

7. A 2013 interview with Steve Zahn presented online using the Oral History Metadata Synchronizer **102**
   Louie B. Nunn Center for Oral History, University of Kentucky Libraries

8. The wall where Marshall A. Webb carved his name on March 30, 1944, in Tremensuoli, Italy **108**
   Photograph by Douglas A. Boyd

Preface

Although I do not remember the specific day, week, or month in 1993, I remember how nervous I was standing on the front porch, hesitating slightly before pressing the doorbell in those moments before conducting my first oral history interview. Everything seemed to move in slow motion. I was a young graduate student researching a paper for a course on the history of Cincinnati, Ohio. I was interviewing people involved in efforts to desegregate a private swim club in the late 1960s. I was about to interview a woman who had initiated those efforts.

My mind was spinning, as I felt entirely overprepared, yet I had this nagging feeling that I was also completely unprepared for what was to come. Having conducted several hours of background research, I knew my research topic and had strategically prepared a sequence of questions that I thought would inspire previously unknown truths. As I pressed the doorbell, my feelings of doubt and insecurity grew. I did not have formal interviewing training. I had no awareness of the vast field and professional practice of oral history or that oral historians worldwide were conducting interviews that were part of small, large, and even global oral history projects. I had no sense that oral history centers and archives were scattered worldwide, preserving and providing access to hundreds of thousands of recorded interviews—primary sources containing unique and invaluable historical data. I simply wanted to learn more about this historical event and record the stories of individuals who had experienced this specific historical moment firsthand.

The moment intensified when the front door opened, and my heart rate rose with excitement. I was greeted with a smile as I entered the home of the woman I'd be interviewing. I had to balance friendly greetings and small talk gracefully while scanning my surroundings for the perfect interview location, where it was quiet yet comfortable and very close to an electric outlet so that I could power my portable tape recorder. We settled on interviewing at the kitchen table. I quickly unpacked the recording equipment, the recorder, the microphones, and the tangled cables that I unwound while making eye contact and nodding in acknowledgment as her stories continued.

What I would have given, at that moment, to have an awareness of professional best practices and a global community of practice. Just as my growing nervousness was on the verge of progressing to a sense of panic, I sat down in the kitchen chair, instinctually made eye contact, and tried to look relaxed. I nervously wondered if the microphones were plugged in and working and if this recorder would actually record my interview. Ignoring the cacophony of thoughts in my mind, I took a deep breath, reached out, and pressed the red record button, and the interview began. I remember these moments so vividly because I relive the experience, in part, almost every time I start a new oral history interview.

I currently direct the Louie B. Nunn Center for Oral History in the University of Kentucky Libraries, a center that has been recording oral histories since 1973. The Nunn Center maintains more than fifty active interviewing initiatives, producing an average of one thousand new interviews a year, and the archive contains over seven hundred oral history projects, resulting in a quickly growing archival collection of more than twenty thousand interviews.

I regularly conduct interviews, train others on interview methodology, and collaborate with project partners to optimize project designs. In addition to working with oral history recording and archival access technologies, I think a great deal about the ethical and legal aspects of conducting and archiving oral history, as well as the theoretical underpinnings of oral history practice.

Like other experienced oral history practitioners, I have interviewed numerous individuals from various backgrounds on an incredibly wide range of topics. I have conducted life story series of interviews, and I have conducted interviews to document historical events. I have interviewed individuals who were poor and wealthy, famous and unknown. I have interviewed musicians, educators, athletes, artists, politicians, factory workers, activists, veterans, entrepreneurs, and broadcasters. I have worked on oral history projects documenting a range of topics, including the civil rights movement in the United States, mental health, partner violence, the bourbon (whiskey) and horse industries, and folk and bluegrass music in Kentucky. I have interviewed individuals from countries around the world, as well as from various communities throughout the United States, including the Navajo Nation, the Appalachian region, and many small neighborhoods. As a former president of the Oral History Association in the United States, I consistently advocate for the national and international oral history practitioner communities. This book draws from over two decades of experience and explores oral history's beauty, complexities, and challenges.

Chapter 1
Tell me a little about yourself

Seated onstage in the Wisconsin Union Theater at the University of Wisconsin–Madison in early September 1954, historian William B. Hesseltine spoke into the microphone. "Ladies and gentlemen, we are assembled here to discuss the worthwhileness of oral history." This statement launched the second session of a colloquium funded by the Rockefeller Foundation called "Ideas in Conflict," held during the annual meeting of the American Association for State and Local History. Four other scholars were on stage with Dr. Hesseltine, whose provocative opening statement would not surprise anyone in the theater that day since the panel was titled "Is Oral History Really Worth While?" Panelists debated the veracity of individual memory, subjectivity, value, and validity as a historical resource. They discussed the great need for standards; they reflected on how expensive oral history at this time could be.

Ultimately, no grand conclusions emerged from these discussions; the skeptics remained skeptics, and the ardent defenders of oral history were undeterred by the naysayers. The final panelist, Professor Fred Shannon from the University of Illinois, was the greatest skeptic on the panel. He began his reflections by stating, "My colleagues have been talking about the reminiscences of old men—and here I am, just another old man standing up here telling you about the unreliability of old men's reminiscences."

But even Shannon left the door open when he went on, "The question is—as the question is stated—Is Oral History Really Worth While? You'll notice the verb 'is'; the question is not 'Will it be some time?'" Certainly, none of the panelists could envision the emergence of a global oral history movement in the coming decades.

This book is about a particular form of history called oral history. In its modern form, oral history is a recorded interview designed to document individual experiences or life stories. It is simultaneously a noun and a verb, a practice, and a historical resource. Oral history is what is wished for after losing a loved one. The recorded voice is what historians often wish for when piecing together silent and material clues asking questions of a historical past that extends beyond living memories. A single interview can begin an oral history project that documents individual lives, communities, and historical events in potentially transformational ways.

In his classic 1978 book, *The Voice of the Past*, historian Paul Thompson reflected on the significance of oral history: "The tape recorder not only allows history to be taken down in spoken words but also presented through them.... The words may be idiosyncratically phrased, but all the more expressive for that. They breathe life into history."

The essence of oral history involves conducting and recording an interview documenting and preserving personal experiences and perspectives and creating greater understanding. In 1927 anthropologist Zora Neale Hurston interviewed Cudjo Lewis, a formerly enslaved person transported from Africa on the last slave ship, the *Clotilda*. In her book, *Barracoon: The Story of the Last "Black Cargo,"* Hurston recalls describing her intentions to Lewis (born Oluale Kossola): "I want to ask you many things. I want to know who you are and how you came to be a slave; and to what part of Africa do you belong, and how you fared as a slave, and how you have managed as a free man?" For centuries the practice of historians focused on the elite and on only those who left behind written and material records. Oral history, by contrast, aligns with an increasing emphasis on social history, preserving and connecting individuals' stories to a broader and more inclusive historical record. Oral history connects individual memories to the community. Just as the idea of "home" and community converts mere space into place, oral history can convert remembrance into resonant understanding and meaning. Oral history involves thoughtful and purposeful project design, an inquisitive interviewer, an audio or video recording device, a narrator, and an archive for preserving and providing access to the recorded interview.

Oral history projects can be large or small. They can be associated with an individual person and span multiple sessions, or they can include single interviews with numerous individuals. A project's scope can be focused on individual biography, a historical event, an organization, or a small community, and a project can span from a local to a national or international scope. A beautiful thing about oral history projects is they can be equally implemented by individuals as well as by small and large institutions.

There are academic oral history centers throughout the world, including the Louie B. Nunn Center for Oral History at the University of Kentucky; Centre for Popular Memory at the University of Cape Town; Baylor University Institute for Oral History; Oral History Program of the University of Buenos Aires (Programa de Historia Oral de la Universidad de Buenos Aires); the Samuel Proctor Oral History Program at the University of Florida; the Oral History Center at the University of California, Berkeley; the Centre for Oral History and Digital Storytelling at Concordia University; the Columbia Center for Oral History at Columbia University; Cui Yongyuan Center for Oral History at the Communication University of China in Beijing; the Oral History Unit and Collective at Newcastle University in Newcastle,

England; the Southern Oral History Program at the University of North Carolina at Chapel Hill; the Center for Oral and Public History at California State University, Fullerton; the University of Wisconsin–Madison Oral History Program; and the Oklahoma Oral History Research Program at Oklahoma State University, to name a few.

Some of these academic oral history institutions focus on recording interviews and hosting projects and initiatives. Some institutions serve as the archive to preserve and provide access to recorded interviews, and others function as both. Some academic oral history institutions focus primarily on training undergraduate and graduate students in interviewing methodologies and interpretive frameworks for oral history, and some of these academic oral history programs, centers, and archives focus primarily on conducting oral history projects with regional, national, and sometimes global missions.

1. A child interviews a coal miner in Kentucky, c. 1981.

Outside of the academic context, there are major oral history projects and archival collections associated with national libraries and archives all over the world, including the British Library; the National Archives of Singapore; the National Archives of the United Arab Emirates Ministry of Presidential Affairs; the National Archive of the Dominican Republic (Archivo General de la Nación); the National Library of New Zealand (Te Puna Mātauranga o Aotearoa); the National Film Video and Sound Archives (a component of the National Archives and Records Service of South Africa); the Centre for Oral History, National and University Library of Iceland; the National Library of Australia; and the Library of Congress in the United States. Many of these national libraries have embarked on large-scale oral history initiatives that interview nationally, such as the Veterans History Project, a volunteer interviewing project hosted by the American Folklife Center at the Library of Congress, which has recorded interviews with military veterans throughout the United States. Other examples include National Life Stories at the British Library and Australian Lives, a national project hosted by the National Library of Australia.

In addition to the work conducted by the dedicated oral history programs, centers, and archives that are currently at the forefront of practice, oral history projects are also being successfully implemented by libraries, museums, large and small companies, state and local historical societies, schools, churches, nonprofit organizations, and even individuals. Some recent examples of oral history work conducted by a range of institutions and organizations include oral history projects by the Brooklyn Historical Society in Brooklyn, New York, including its award-winning Crossing Borders, Bridging Generations Oral History Project, which conducted life history interviews with more than one hundred narrators from the Brooklyn community. According to the project description, interview topics included self and identity; religion and tradition; laws and mores; food and celebration; love and marriage; parents and children; race and ethnicity; and cultural preservation. The Southern Foodways Alliance (SFA) in Mississippi hosts a range of oral history projects documenting various aspects of food and culture in the southern United States. The SFA project Career Servers Oral History Project records life story interviews with individuals "who built careers waiting tables in New Orleans, Louisiana; Charleston, South Carolina; and Atlanta, Georgia." The Memories of Brazilians Project (Projeto Memórias dos Brasileiros) was launched by the Museo da Pessoa in Brazil to record the life stories of Brazilians, focusing on documenting social and cultural changes in Brazil. The Cork Folklore Project in Cork, Ireland, was established to record the memories and stories of community residents. The Act Up Oral History Project in New York City interviewed members of Act Up (AIDS Coalition to Unleash Power), a grassroots activist organization working to end the AIDS pandemic. In Owensboro, Kentucky, the Bluegrass Music Hall of Fame and Museum, formerly known as the International Bluegrass Music Museum (IBMM), launched an oral history project to document the first generation of bluegrass music, resulting in a project that contains over 150 video-recorded oral history interviews documenting the history of bluegrass music. Averaging two to three hours, these interviews include life stories of many musicians known as bluegrass music's first generation, covering a range of topics pertaining to their lives as artists and performers.

Several major oral history initiatives were created outside the traditional realms of academia, libraries and archives, and public history. In 1994 iconic film director Steven Spielberg established the Shoah Foundation to record and preserve oral history interviews conducted with Holocaust survivors and witnesses, culminating in over 57,000 interviews (conducted on professionally recorded video) with individuals in forty-five different languages representing seventy countries of origin. Now associated with the University of Southern California, the USC Shoah Foundation expanded to utilize oral history to document genocide in countries worldwide.

Inspired by the work of the Shoah Foundation, Densho: The Japanese American Legacy Project was launched in Seattle, Washington, in 1996 to record and preserve interviews that documented the incarceration of Japanese Americans in the United States during World War II. The Densho project contains more than nine hundred interviews, as well as archived letters, photographs, newspaper clippings, and other materials that have been digitized and made available online. In an interview conducted with Sharon Tanagi Aburano by Tom Ikeda on April 3, 2008, archived as part of the Densho Visual History Collection, Aburano reflects on first seeing her mother's emotional reaction to the internment camps:

IKEDA: So let's go back, so you're just finishing the vaccinations, and then…

TANAGI ABURANO: Yes, and then they told us to—this was the only place that this ever happened—to pick up our bags and fill it with straw for the mattress, and that's the first time I saw my mother's tears. To be reduced to that, I think, was just too much for her to bear or something. But she had never broken down, and I was just amazed. But it is demeaning to have to fill up your [bed mattress with straw]. Up to this time, I thought, you know, the Japanese are full of pride and dignity, but this was too much [for her] to bear.

IKEDA: So, how did that feel for you? You're what, about sixteen years old?

TANAGI ABURANO: I was fifteen going on sixteen, because I turned sixteen in October and we were in May that year.

IKEDA: And then to see your, your mother sort of break down for the first time…

TANAGI ABURANO: Yeah, I was (shocked), because as I said, on December 7th, when my father and mother heard about Pearl Harbor, they were ashen-faced but not a word came out of 'em about anything. But like I said, that's a Japanese virtue. They don't want to talk about problems or illness of any type.

Although there are numerous oral history projects that document US presidencies and world leaders, and the lives and the careers of successful, and elite, individuals, oral history excels most when documenting the lives and experiences of those who would be, otherwise, left out of the historical record.

Featured oral history projects

The following is a selection of some current or recent examples of interviewing projects documenting historical perspectives not reflected in the "official" historical record:

Bringing Them Home Oral History Project	National Library of Australia
Voces Oral History Project	The University of Texas at Austin
The Women in Bourbon (Whiskey) Oral History Project	Louie B. Nunn Center for Oral History, University of Kentucky Libraries
NHS at 70: The Story of Our Lives	The Centre for the History of Science, Technology and Medicine, University of Manchester
Mississippi Freedom Project	Samuel Proctor Oral History Program, University of Florida
Queer Newark Oral History Project	Rutgers University–Newark
History of the Black Movement in Brazil	Centro de Pesquisa e Documentação de História Contemporânea do Brasil (The Center for Research and Documentation of Contemporary History of Brazil) of the Getulio Vargas Foundation in Rio de Janeiro (CPDOC)

The Palestinian Oral History Archive	American University of Beirut
The Rule of Law Oral History Project	Columbia Center for Oral History, Columbia University
Rosie the Riveter WWII American Homefront Oral History Project	National Park Service, the City of Richmond, and the Oral History Center, University of California, Berkeley
Regional Memory and Image Before the Great East Japan Earthquake	University of Tsukaba, Keio University
Delhi Oralities Project	Centre of Community Knowledge (CCK), Dr. B. R. Ambedkar University Delhi

In the pre-Internet age, the highest-profile popular outputs of oral history tended to be linked to radio, some scattered television documentaries, and books. Some of the highest-profile radio examples include Studs Terkel's long-form interview programs on WFMT in Chicago (many of which are now available streaming online), as well as public radio documentaries such as the *Working Lives* series produced by folklorist Brenda McCallum and the *I Remember When: Times Gone but Not Forgotten* and *Goin' North: Tales of the Great Migration* documentaries produced by oral historian Charles Hardy. There have been numerous examples over the years of best-selling and popular books that utilized oral history methodology, including Terkel's *Hard Times: An Oral History of the Great Depression*, initially published in 1970; *American Journey: The Times of Robert Kennedy*, featuring interviews by Jean Stein and edited by George Plimpton, published in 1970; *Plain Speaking: An Oral Biography of Harry S. Truman*, written by Merle Miller and published in 1972; *The Foxfire Book: Hog Dressing, Log Cabin Building, Mountain Crafts and Foods, Planting by the Signs, Snake Lore, Hunting Tales, Faith Healing, Moonshining, and Other Affairs of*

Plain Living, edited by Eliot Wigginton and first published in 1972; and *Please Kill Me Now: An Uncensored Oral History of Punk*, by Leggs McNeil and Gillian McClain, published in 1996.

Since the early 2000s, the proliferation of portable digital audio and video recorders and cameras and the Internet's maturing into the Web 2.0 era, characterized by social media, the podcast, and streaming audio and video, have significantly elevated awareness of oral history. The practice of oral history gained recognition both in academia and public history contexts and in public consciousness and popular culture. Journalist Tom Brokaw's best-selling 1998 book, *The Greatest Generation*, cast a high-profile spotlight on veterans' stories, sparking a movement to interview World War II veterans. In 2000 the US Congress established the Veterans History Project as part of the American Folklife Center at the Library of Congress to document the experiences of military veterans in all branches of service ranging from World War I to the more recent conflicts.

Following the September 11, 2001, terrorist attacks on the World Trade Center in New York City, numerous institutions, including Columbia University, Stony Brook University, Pace University, and the National Park Service, launched major oral history projects documenting various aspects of the tragedy from multiple perspectives. Following Hurricane Katrina's devastating impact on New Orleans in 2005, dozens of institutions launched oral history projects, including the Historic New Orleans Collection, Louisiana State University's T. Harry Williams Center for Oral History, and University of Southern Mississippi.

In addition to conducting oral history interviews, individuals around the world began to access and listen to interviews conducted by others. Archived oral history interviews are now regularly featured on the radio, in museum exhibits, in classrooms at all levels, in documentaries, and in podcast episodes. Oral history is widely presented in the form of short-form articles throughout the internet and print-based journalism. There is an increased interdisciplinary output in more traditional scholarly publications, as well as an increasing presence in both academic and popular books.

In 2015 Belarusian writer Svetlana Alexievich won the Nobel Prize for Literature for her book *Voices from Chernobyl,* based on oral history interviews she conducted documenting the 1986 nuclear disaster. Alexievich interviewed witnesses that included first responders, members of the clean-up team, politicians, doctors, firefighters, and community members affected by the radiation. She won acclaim for what the Nobel Prize announcement described as a "polyphonic" use of testimony and characterized this oral history-based book as "a monument to suffering and courage in our time." The popular HBO series *Chernobyl* was largely based on Alexievich's writings and oral history interviews.

For more than a century, oral history has been practiced by folklorists, anthropologists, and historians focused on academic and scholarly inquiry across the humanities and social sciences within academia. Outside of academia and traditional scholarship, oral history methodology is now actively used by journalists, activists, authors, documentarians, podcasters, teachers and students, producers, museum curators, genealogists, librarians, archivists, neighbors, community leaders, and family members. As a practice, oral history is experiencing an explosive phase of growth, and new initiatives to document and record the history of a person, a place, an institution, a movement, a historical event, or a community are utilizing oral history methodology on a global scale.

Going more deeply into the mission of expanding the archival and historical record, oral history has had a transformational impact, documenting the individual experiences and the memories of underrepresented, neglected, and marginalized communities worldwide. Oral history can amplify voices once ignored by the historical record and assist in processing and creating historical understandings of trauma, as was the case in the Bringing Them Home Oral History Project conducted by the National Library of Australia between 1998 and 2002. This oral history project, which conducted 340 interviews, was a direct response to the *National Inquiry into the Separation of Aboriginal and Torres Strait Islander Children from Their Families* report, a national inquiry into the "Stolen Generations" policies of forced removal of Aboriginal and Torres Strait Islander children. The project recorded powerful stories of Indigenous people and interviewed officials and administrators, as well as the police, hospital staff, and missionaries involved in the process. The impact of this oral history project extended beyond historical documentation, creating a space for cultural healing and historical validation and creating a solid platform for advocacy and the call for future policy changes.

Oral history can function as an important component in community healing processes and historical reconciliation practices in post-conflict environments, as demonstrated by its intentional role in documenting and striving for a deeper understanding of the human impact of apartheid in South Africa. The South African History Project (SAHP) directly integrated oral history into public school curricula; the South African History Archive (SAHA) launched several projects to record firsthand accounts and to document the impact of apartheid; and the South African Democracy Education Trust (SADET) Oral History Project trained educators in oral history methods and provided training on designing oral history projects that would enhance the curriculum.

Beginning in 2006, Taylor Krauss, founder of the Voices of Rwanda Archive, conducted hundreds of video-recorded interviews with Rwandans to document the genocide and to, as the *Christian Science Monitor* described in 2008, "help the country heal with history." Krauss later articulated that his intention for the oral history project was to "build a bridge toward a deeper understanding of the hearts and minds of those dehumanized by genocide." Oral history, both the interviewing practice and the results of a project, can actively promote anti-oppression and social justice, as shown by the collaborative and community-based work of Voice of Witness, a human rights organization in the United States that publishes an extensive series of publications and resources on utilizing oral history.

In 1964 the American author and poet Robert Penn Warren conducted oral history interviews with civil rights movement leaders for a book called *Who Speaks for the Negro?* (1965), which included interviews with Martin Luther King Jr., Malcolm X, Stokely Carmichael, Andrew Young, James Baldwin, Reverand Ralph Abernathy, James Famer, Vernon Jordan, Whitney Young, and many others. In December 1964 Warren donated forty-three of these interviews to the Nunn Center at the University of Kentucky. Warren listed the interviews in his donation letter dated December 23, 1964, and commented, "This, it would seem, is significant research material." Oral history is, indeed, significant. And it has proven, without a doubt, to be worthwhile.

Chapter 2
Defining oral history through time

On November 11, 1773, biographer James Boswell wrote in his travel journal, documenting a trip through Scotland with his friend, English writer Samuel Johnson, about their discussion on the nature of history, narrative, and impartiality. According to Boswell, Johnson proclaimed, "A man, by talking with those of different sides, who were actors in it, and putting down all that he hears, may in time collect the materials of a good narrative. You are to consider, all history was at first oral." As contemporary historians Paul Thompson and Joanna Bornat put it, "Oral history is as old as history itself. It was the first kind of history." People have relied on stories to better understand and gain insight into the past we call history, historical events, and the shared human experience since long before recorded history.

The word "history" is derived from the Greek word *historia*, which is derived from the Greek verb *historein*, meaning to learn by inquiry. Contemporary perception of oral history is a methodology, a practice, and a field of study rooted in the act of intentional inquiry—asking questions, listening to others, recording, and remembering. There have been many attempts to define and redefine oral history through the years, and the definitions will continue to change. Historian Linda Shopes has stated that oral history is a "maddeningly imprecise term" that can accurately refer to many different things, and historian Charles

Morrissey declared, "Oral history is mulish. Stubbornly, it resists a unifying terminology." The meanings signified when someone uses the phrase "oral history" today are, indeed, wide-ranging. Of course, words and their meanings change through time and depend greatly on cultural and historical contexts. There is no single definition of oral history through time; even today, it remains fluid and dynamic.

Although contemporary oral history practice had numerous points of origin, the most common origin story of the contemporary academic oral history movement in the United States is attributed to historian Allan Nevins, who established the Columbia Center for Oral History at Columbia University in 1948. The Columbia Center represents the first institutionalization of the practice of what would become known as "oral history." Ten years prior, Nevins proposed in the introduction to his book *Gateway to History*, "some organization which made a systematic attempt to obtain, from the lips and papers of living Americans who had led significant lives, a fuller record of their participation in the political, economic, and cultural life of the last sixty years." Most oral history projects in the United States between the early 1950s and the 1960s emulated various aspects of the Columbia model, including a focus on interviewing elite figures in politics, business, science, and culture, and emphasizing professional standards that included more standardized interviewing techniques, release forms, and transcription standards and style guides.

Likewise, the dominant conceptualization defining oral history at this time was largely influenced by the discussions among the individuals who met in September 1966, for the First National Colloquium on Oral History, a meeting at Lake Arrowhead, California, that formally became the Oral History Association the following year. The individuals attending and presenting at this meeting practiced oral history in various contexts and included archivists and librarians, folklorists, historians, genealogists, medical doctors, and even psychiatrists. Although one of the first panels was titled "Definitions of Oral History," the conversations across the next few days all grappled with defining oral history. Panelists and presenters spoke about differentiating oral history from the practice of folklorists and journalists. There was a lot of discussion about what did not constitute oral history, such as recorded speeches or news broadcasts. There were spirited and provocative discussions trying to define and professionalize this emerging practice. In some ways, these conversations and debates continue today.

Just as the First National Colloquium tried to clearly define oral history, countless contemporary oral history publications or manuals typically begin with a definition. In her 1969 publication, *Oral History for the Local Historical Society*, historian Willa Baum stated:

> Oral history is the tape-recording of reminiscences about which the narrator can speak from first-hand knowledge. Through pre-planned interviews, the information is captured in question and answer form by oral history interviewers. The interviewer must have some background knowledge of the subject and considerable social skill in knowing how to draw the narrator out. Oral history is not the tape-recording of speeches.

In the article "Directions for Oral History in the U.S.," historian Ronald J. Grele of Columbia describes oral history as "the interviewing of eye-witness participants in the events of the past for the purposes of historical reconstruction." In the 1988 publication *Memories & Reflections*, the National Archives of Singapore begins by defining oral history as follows:

> The systematic collection of memories and knowledge about historical events and periods by researchers and institutions conducting recorded interviews with selected narrators. The recorded information is then preserved for posterity and made

available for research purposes. It is one way of recording history that cuts across all strata of society, thereby enriching our knowledge of human experiences across space and time.

Donald A. Ritchie begins his influential book *Doing Oral History* with the canonical definition:

> An oral history interview generally consists of a well-prepared interviewer questioning an interviewee and recording their exchange in audio or video format. Recordings of the interview are transcribed, summarized, or indexed and then placed in a library or archives. These interviews may be used for research or excerpted in a publication, radio or video documentary, museum exhibition, dramatization, or other form of public presentation. Recordings, transcripts, catalogs, photographs, and related documentary materials are often posted on websites. Oral history does not include random or surreptitious recordings, nor does it refer to recorded speeches, wiretapping, personal diaries on tape, or other sound recordings that lack the dialogue between interviewer and interviewee.

However, the history of oral history—the term and the practice—extends back far beyond Allan Nevins and the establishment of the Columbia Center for Oral History in 1948 and far beyond the borders of the United States. In fact, the roots of oral history practice extend back even before the advent of audio recording; the roots even extend beyond the professional practice of historians.

Stories of the past, stories of place, and origin stories were told, and they were retold, circulating in many forms, remembered, and passed down through generations before being written down and published. Two principal textualized examples of this process include the Bible and the Qur'an. These sacred texts consist of stories first circulated through oral tradition by the followers of Jesus and Muhammad and eventually written down.

Not coincidentally, the word "Qur'an" is rooted in the Arabic word meaning "the Recitation." The Prophet Muhammad orally conveyed the divine revelations, which his companions memorized verbatim and eventually compiled decades after his death in 632 CE. Contemporary research identifies Homer's *Odyssey* and *Iliad* as works derived from oral poetry, which were orally performed, remembered, reperformed, and passed down through generations before eventually being written down.

Folklorists classify traditional stories into a myriad of forms and narrative genres that include myth and legend as well as folk and fairy tales, but it is the stories that emerge from personal memories and life experiences that create the foundation of one's sense of self and personal identity. When those stories are remembered and repeated, they move through time and space; the individual is connected to the community, and a common cultural frame of reference emerges from stories about the past. Stories about the past take many forms, including legends, myths or sacred narratives, origin stories, poetry, ballads, folk music, and lyrics. When stories of many forms are told and remembered, these stories become part of history and community memory; they become part of what is often referred to as "oral tradition," "folk history," or, sometimes, the "tradition of the country."

The earliest printed uses of the phrase "oral history" were references to stories passed down through generations in the form of oral tradition. In his 1725 publication of *A Tour Thro' the Whole Island of Great Britain, Divided into Circuits or Journies. Giving a Particular and Diverting Account of Whatever Is Curious, and Worth Observation*, Daniel Defoe wrote about Tintagel Castle:

> As for the Story of King Arthur being both born and killed there, 'tis a Piece of Tradition, only on Oral History, and not any Authority to be produced for it.

Often implied in the early usages of "oral history" was an unverifiable and, potentially, untrue traditional version of history. In an 1809 article published in the *Belfast Monthly Magazine* titled "An Account of Island Magee," the author mentions, "At the west end, as you enter the island, is a small rivulet called Slaughter ford, from the massacre of 1642, which oral history says began here." The author of the 1827 article "Indians of the Northwestern Frontier" in the *Adams Sentinel* in Gettysburg, Pennsylvania, speculates on the origins of the Shawnee Native American tribe, stating "the actual identity of language furnishes irrefragable proof, and the incidents of the separation yet live in the oral history of each tribe." An 1834 article appeared in the *Dublin Penny Journal* titled "A Guide to the Giants' Causeway," noting, "Oral history states, that 'in olden time' all the rents of Ireland were paid at this place, and that the last Danish invaders embarked from here."

When the Western conceptualization of oral tradition was signified by the phrase "oral history," the reference implied an informal corpus of stories about the past, often associated with a particular community or culture, preserved in collective memory, told, retold, and remembered by the community historians and performers, and passed down orally through generations. This early form of "oral history" was almost entirely associated with the stories representing communities and cultures whose histories were not documented or expressed in written form; therefore, they were outside of the scope of written or "official" history, at least until the stories were eventually written down. The problem with this distinction is the exclusionary assumption that if narratives are never "written down," they could not be considered formal or legitimate history. This exclusion was clearly articulated by anthropologist Robert Lowie in 1916 during his address to the American Folklore Society's annual meeting. As the outgoing president, he delivered what folklorist Richard Dorson later characterized as "the strongest statement against traditional history on this side of the Atlantic": "Indian tradition is historically worthless... because the occurrences, possibly real, which it retains, are of no historical significance; and because it fails to record, or to record accurately, the most momentous happenings."

Beginning in the late nineteenth century, as disciplinary boundaries were constructed in the academy and academic fields drew lines to differentiate theory and practice, oral narratives were perceived by most of the professional history community as unreliable, and they were ignored as valid primary sources. This dichotomy was eloquently described by Dorson as a "rigid polarization between history as scrupulously documented fact, and folklore as unverified rumor, falsehood, hearsay, old wives' tales—often equated with myth and legend." Oral tradition became the focus of folklorists and anthropologists, and the written document became the focus of most historians.

As practice and methodologies are professionalized and transition into fields, there is often the impulse for practitioners, especially within academia, to create methodological and theoretical divisions and disciplines. The professionalization of history is often attributed to German historian Leopold von Ranke, who advocated in the late nineteenth century for more evidence-based and scientific historical practice, a practice that was rooted in documents and facts. As late as 1962, English historian Hugh Trevor-Roper declared, "Perhaps in the future, there will be some African history to teach. But at the present there is none—there is only the history of the Europeans in Africa. The rest is darkness... and darkness is not a subject of history." This now-discarded view represented typical disdain for oral sources. However, even the early Greek historians struggled greatly with the notion of veracity in eyewitness testimony. Overcoming the exclusionary question of reliability and veracity has been an ongoing challenge for professional oral history practice that continues today. Historians shunning oral tradition inevitably excluded and marginalized entire cultures in a state of what anthropologist Marshall Sahlins called "historylessness."

In the mid-twentieth century, the perceived limitations posed by veracity and reliability in oral history—especially in the definitional context of oral tradition—began to shift radically. In the 1956 article "The Problem of Traditional History with Special Reference to Yoruba Traditions" published in the *Journal of the Historical Society of Nigeria*, Nigerian historian Saburi Biobaku wrote:

> THE HISTORIAN of a non-literate people cannot afford to ignore the traditional accounts of the people's past. He must delve into traditional history, which is essentially *remembered history*, handed down from one generation to another. The technique of African traditional history is constantly to keep alive the memory of the past; to preserve the past consciously in the present.

With the 1961 publication of *De la tradition orale* and the 1985 publication of *Oral Tradition as History*, Belgian historian Jan Vansina revolutionized historical perceptions of oral tradition, establishing an interdisciplinary model for understanding and valuing oral tradition in the professional interpretation and analysis of "history."

In all cultures, words and their meanings are in a continuous state of change. The early Western concept of "oral history" equated to what is now perceived by the mainstream as "oral tradition," a corpus of stories created in that imagined time before writing when stories were passed down orally, resulting in a corpus of remembered and retold tales of the past. Although the Western concept of history is dominated by what has been "written" rather than what has been "told," oral tradition is very much part of the traditional roots and the lineage of the contemporary field and practice of oral history. As one traces the more modern history of oral history practice, the interview emerges as a critical definitional element differentiating "oral history" and "oral tradition"—the intentional act of one individual asking questions of another individual and recording the spoken accounts of their lived experiences, their eyewitness accounts, their perceptions and understandings of their past.

The interview as a defining component

Numerous historians of oral history's methodological roots reference interviews conducted in the fifth century BCE by Herodotus, documenting the history of the Persian Wars, and Thucydides, who conducted eyewitness interviews for his book *History of the Peloponnesian Wars*, as early examples of oral history interviewing. Thucydides wrote about the value of interviewing eyewitnesses and reflected on the challenges of relying solely upon oral sources: "And with reference to the narrative of events, far from permitting myself to derive it from the first source that came to hand, I did not even trust my own impressions, but it rests partly on what I saw myself, partly on what others saw for me."

Similarly, historians of the practice of oral history cite numerous examples when "interviewing" people was the principal methodology for documenting experiences and understanding the past. In the second century BCE, a scribe and historian for the Han dynasty in China, Sima Qian, interviewed "the elders" to preserve stories for *Records of the Grand Historian* or *Shi Ji*, an epic publication documenting the history of ancient China. Around 731 CE, Venerable Bede, a Benedictine monk, author of *Ecclesiastical History of the English People*, wrote: "I received not on the authority of any one man, but by the faithful testimony of innumerable witnesses, who might know or remember the same; besides what I had of my own knowledge."

Between 1540 and 1590, Bernardino de Sahagún, a Spanish Franciscan friar serving as a missionary in what is now known as Mexico, systematically documented Aztec history, religion, language, and culture. Sahagún learned the Aztec language Nahuatl, collaborated with Indigenous communities, collected oral testimony, and eventually produced *Historia general de las Cosas de Nueva España*, a manuscript of more than 2,400 pages of text and images organized in twelve books. Book Twelve documents the Spanish-led conquest of Tenochtitlan from the Indigenous perspective. In 1751 the French Enlightenment writer, philosopher, and historian Voltaire, who had expressed skepticism of oral tradition and fables as history, utilized eyewitness accounts to write his *Le Siècle de Louis XIV*. Historian Jules Michelet used oral testimony for his monumental seven-volume *Historical View of the French Revolution*, published between 1847 and 1855, citing sources that were "gathered from the lips of old men."

On March 6, 1821, John Fanning Watson, an amateur historian and antiquarian from Philadelphia, wrote a letter to *Poulson's American Daily Advertiser* advocating for interviewing as a methodology. He opined, "I have often thought our old inhabitants might give many interesting facts respecting the times in which they were young." In Watson's personal journal, which he titled *Trip to Reading 1825*, Watson drafted a series of interview questions he labeled "Queries of Aged Persons in Philadelphia." The questions were designed to document personal recollections and eyewitness accounts and descriptions of his city. Question #23, for instance, asked, "What were the most remarkable events within your memory?" and question #26, "What did you think of British Army and Navy officers before the war?" Watson interviewed several individuals for his research, and in 1829 he produced the first edition of *Annals of Philadelphia, Being a Collection of Memoirs, Anecdotes, & Incidents of the City and Its Inhabitants*. Watson's interview technique was documented in Deborah Norris Logan's diary entry from March 17, 1827:

> We drank tea and had a great deal of amusing chat, he constantly recurring to the "olden time," asks me questions which bring back the memory of departed and altered things, and elicits much that he likes to be acquainted with,—in this way he does to others and obtains such a map (but in its present state it is an heterogeneous one) of information.

In the late 1830s, collector, archivist, historian, and antiquarian Lyman C. Draper began to write letters to the aging generation of Kentucky pioneers, asking questions about their early frontier experiences. By 1843, Draper set out on the first of many research and collection trips to interview Western pioneers and "rescue" their histories, writing, "very much precious historical incident must still be treasured up in the memory of aged Western Pioneers, which would perish with them if not quickly rescued." In 1953 Draper's biographer William B. Hesseltine described him as "an expert interviewer." In his 1903 book, *How George Rogers Clark Won the Northwest and Other Essays in Western History*, Reuben Gold Thwaites reflected on Draper and his interviewing methodology, describing Draper as "the guest of the 'interviewed,'" an "inquisitive stranger" who visited the pioneers' homes "in the New York, Ohio, Kentucky, Virginia, and Tennessee backwoods—long enough to extract with the acquired skill of a cross-examiner, every morsel of historical information, every item of valuable reminiscence stored in the mind of his host."

In parallel with Draper, the Reverend John Dabney Shane, a Presbyterian minister in Lexington, Kentucky, conducted more than three hundred interviews in the 1840s and 1850s with early pioneers in Kentucky, Ohio, and Pennsylvania, documenting their firsthand memories and recollections about everyday frontier life. Shane's transcribed interviews and writings were purchased in 1863 by Lyman Copeland Draper and became part of the Draper manuscript collection at the Wisconsin Historical Society.

Another early interviewer, William Still, was a free-born Black businessman and abolitionist in Philadelphia. In 1847 he was hired as the clerk for the Pennsylvania Society for the Abolition of Slavery, and he later became active in the Underground Railroad, directly assisting hundreds of enslaved individuals to escape slavery in the South. In addition to keeping meticulous records, Still interviewed many of the individuals he assisted, culminating in the 1872 publication *The Underground Railroad: Authentic Narratives and First-Hand Accounts*, which included hundreds of individual first-person narratives that provided rare and detailed accounts of their personal experiences escaping from slavery.

Beginning in the 1870s, historian, collector, and publisher Hubert Howe Bancroft and his staff launched a major initiative to interview hundreds of pioneers to the American West to document what Bancroft called dictations or "old-timer" tales. These interviews were a major source for the thirty-nine volumes of history that he published between 1874 and 1890. Starting in 1888 and continuing into the 1920s, James Stuart, a civil servant in the southern African British colonies of Zululand and Natal, interviewed more than two hundred individuals documenting the history and culture of the Zulu. Stuart, a fluent Zulu speaker, conducted interviews in both English and Zulu. The interviews were eventually published posthumously as a five-volume set between 1976 and 2021 as *The James Stuart Archive of Recorded Oral Evidence Relating to the History of the Zulu and Neighboring Peoples*.

In the mid- to late nineteenth century, a large-scale movement emerged that was led by American and European folklorists and ethnographers to intentionally preserve aspects of cultures that were perceived as disappearing, especially focusing efforts on documenting North American Indigenous cultures. Practitioners rigorously focused effort and resources on preserving language, songs, stories, and myth, as well as cultural traditions and other forms of artistic expression. In 1879 the US government established the Bureau of Ethnology, later renamed the Bureau of American Ethnology (BAE) in 1897. The BAE, a division of the Smithsonian Institution, became the principal organizer and sponsor of anthropological work documenting and preserving Native American cultures on a large scale. Out of this movement emerged the roots of modern anthropology, led by anthropologist Franz Boas, who emphasized the importance of ethnographic fieldwork, traveling to the community being studied, directly observing, and talking to individuals through formal interviewing. Boas extensively documented narrative texts as he worked with the Tsimshian, the Chinook, and the Kwakiutl, but his students, including A. L. Kroeber, Edward Sapir, Margaret Mead, Ruth Benedict, and Zora Neale Hurston, conducted ethnographic interviews worldwide.

Until the 1870s, the practice of interviewing individuals as a methodology for documenting first-hand experiences and recollections universally manifested in the form of field notes, written transcription, and print documents. However, in 1877 the inventor Thomas Alva Edison created the technology to record and preserve the human voice. In 1878 Edison wrote the article "The Phonograph and Its Future" for the *North American Review*, speculating on future applications of his recording technology:

> For the purpose of preserving the sayings, the voices, and the last words of the dying member of the family—as of great men—the phonograph will unquestionably outrank the photograph.... It will henceforth be possible to preserve for future generations the voices as well as the words of our Washingtons, our Lincolns, our Gladstones, etc., and to have them give us their "greatest effort" in every town and hamlet in the country, upon our holidays.

The April 19, 1878, edition of the Washington, DC, *Evening Star* reported Edison's appearance at the National Academy of Sciences the day before. The article recounted Edison's remarks about the potential use of the phonograph for fieldwork by ethnologists:

> I saw the president of the American Philological Society the other day.... He wants one of my improved phonographs to preserve the accents of the Onandagas and Tuscaroras who are dying out. One old man speaks the language fluently and correctly, and he is afraid it will die.... The phonograph will preserve the exact pronunciation.

In 1890 anthropologist and writer J. Walter Fewkes is believed by many to be the first to utilize the phonograph to record interviews with Indigenous people when he conducted several recording sessions with Passamaquoddy in Maine, recording on wax cylinders.

In the years following, numerous ethnographers, anthropologists, folklorists, linguists, and ethnomusicologists, including Fewkes, Franz Boas, Paul Radin, Elsie Clews Parsons, Helen Heffrom Roberts, Frances Densmore, and Alice Cunningham Fletcher, utilized this recording technology to record interviews with individuals representing Indigenous peoples and communities around North America. Most of the interviews recorded during this period were folkloristic, focusing on the performance of specific stories, specific songs, and the discussion of specific traditions. For example, the anthropologist and linguist John Peabody Harrington, who began working for the BAE in 1915, meticulously and comprehensively documented the language and cultures, including the Kiowa, Chumash, Yuma, Mojave, Kitanemuk, and Serrano. Harrington's primary motivation was documenting and preserving languages, and he often sought out the last speakers of languages. From this era of ethnographic interviewers, Harrington's interviews closely resemble the contemporary oral history interview, including life histories and personal reminiscences, in addition to traditional cultural information and performance.

2. John Peabody Harrington, an ethnologist working for the Bureau of American Ethnology, interviews Margarita (Marguerite) Compos, a member of the Guna community, 1924.

At the midpoint of the Great Depression in 1935, US President Franklin D. Roosevelt launched the Federal Writers Project, a New Deal initiative that would employ thousands of people into the early 1940s. The Federal Writers Project hired writers, artists, folklorists, anthropologists, and historians to produce numerous publications, including city and state guidebooks, and to conduct thousands of oral history interviews documenting the life histories of ordinary individuals. Many of these interviews were conducted under the direction of folklorist Benjamin Botkin, who served as the national folklore editor from 1938 to 1941 and later became the head of the Archive of Folk Song at the Library of Congress. Botkin charged these interviewers to "make your informant feel important. Well-conducted interviews serve as social occasions to which informants come to look forward." The Federal Writers Project was responsible for conducting nearly ten thousand oral history interviews throughout the United States and employed numerous individuals who later rose significantly in prominence, including Richard Wright, Zora Neale Hurston, Ralph Ellison, Saul Bellow, Anzia Yezierska, Studs Terkel, Stetson Kennedy, and Arna Bontemps.

Most significantly, the Federal Writers Project was responsible for conducting interviews with formerly enslaved individuals. Commenting on the interview guidelines for "Stories from Ex-Slaves," folklorist John Lomax, an advisor to the Federal Writers Project in 1937, wrote: "The main purpose of these detailed and homely questions is to get the Negro interested in talking about the days of slavery." Later known as the Slave Narrative Collection archived at the Library of Congress, the initiative resulted in more than two thousand interviews documenting enslaved individuals' firsthand experiences. To this day, this collection of interviews represents one of the rarest and most important oral history projects ever conducted.

In 1942, during World War II, Forrest C. Pogue was drafted into the US Army and served as a master sergeant in the Historical Division of the War Department. A historian prior to the war, Pogue and a small group of combat historians were charged with documenting and historically contextualizing the war experience to produce pamphlets that could be provided to the wounded or to families of those killed in action. On June 6, 1944, Pogue accompanied the troops on the D-Day invasion of Normandy. Using a magnetic wire recorder, Pogue conducted dozens of interviews with wounded soldiers in the days and weeks following the D-Day invasion and later interviewed soldiers involved in the Battle of the Bulge. Pogue is acknowledged as a pioneer of battlefield-style oral history interviewing and was awarded the Bronze Star and the Croix de Guerre for his "front line" interviewing.

In December 1944 a small group of Jewish historians formed the Jewish Historical Institute in Poland. Formed in Lublin just months following the liberation of the Majdanek concentration camp, the group created an archive to document and preserve the personal experiences and trauma of the Holocaust. Several historical commissions throughout Europe were formed shortly thereafter, and they focused their collecting efforts on archiving diaries, documents, and photographs, as well as launching an interviewing initiative to record individual witness testimonies. Between 1944 and 1949, the Jewish Historical Institute, the Hungarian National Relief Committee for Deportees, and the German Central Historical Commission conducted more than thirteen thousand interviews. Most interviews were recorded only in writing; however, in 1946, David Boder, an American professor of psychology, traveled to Europe and conducted 130 interviews with Jewish survivors (in nine different languages), which he recorded using a wire audio recorder. In subsequent years, Boder would publish numerous books and articles, including *I Did Not Interview the Dead* (1949), based on these interviews, which represent some of the earliest audio-recorded interviews documenting the Holocaust.

In 1948 Nigerian historian Kenneth Onwuka Dike traveled back to Nigeria for a six-month research trip to conduct oral history interviews for his doctoral dissertation at the University of London; it was eventually published as *Trade and Politics in the Niger Delta, 1830–1885* in 1956. Dike's influential interdisciplinary methodology expanded research of African and Nigerian history beyond the sole usage of colonial written records and introduced interviewing, oral tradition, archaeology, and linguistics to decolonize the African historical record.

Historian Allan Nevins, who recognized the importance of interviewing methodology in the practice of history as early as the late 1930s, is commonly credited with semantically connecting "oral history" with the practice of interviewing when he established the Columbia Center for Oral History in 1948. At that time, numerous formal and informal interviewing initiatives worldwide were being conducted for various documentary and research purposes. However, it is unknown if anyone referred to this interviewing practice as "oral history." The multidisciplinary practice of conducting life history interviews to record and document firsthand experiences or witnessed events to expand, enhance, and individualize the historical record and create greater cultural and historical understanding was growing.

Historians interested in tracing the practice of oral history have attempted to identify some of the earliest instances when the term "oral history" was semantically transformed from denoting the stories of oral tradition into a formal and intentional practice involving interviewing. In 1980 historian Charles T. Morrissey wrote an article entitled "Why Call It 'Oral History'? Searching for Early Usage of a Generic Term," in which he documented his research into the evolution of the term. Acknowledging Nevins in 1948, Morrissey recounts a discovery he made while conducting research for a book on the history of Vermont. Morrisey recalls reading a paper presented by Winslow Cossoul Watson during a meeting of the Vermont Historical Society in 1863. Watson, a historian, praised the Vermont Historical Society for its active approach to "Garner up the authentic legends and traditions of prominent men and preserve the records of their transactions.... I have been amazed by observing in my own local researches the ravages made by a single decade, among the fountains of oral history in a community." Morrissey then observes Watson's advocacy for interviewing as the recommended methodology.

But the term was used two years earlier in 1861 by the Arctic explorer Charles Francis Hall in an entry in his personal journal in which he describes his interviews of local Inuit people as "oral history." Hall, a newspaper publisher in Cincinnati, Ohio, had become obsessed with solving the mystery of the 1845 vanishing of two English ships commanded by Sir John Franklin that set sail to the Canadian Arctic on a quest to find the fabled Northwest Passage. When the ships and crew did not return and were presumed missing, Franklin's wife had offered a £3,000 reward, and in 1849, the British government announced a £20,000 reward, enticing numerous dangerous expeditions that yielded some clues, but none that were definitive. In 1860 a determined Charles Francis Hall secured passage on a whaling vessel to try to solve the mystery. Attempting to piece together clues, Hall documents a particular interview: "While Koo-too-ne-ung ("Gary") was boiling my coffee I had an interview with Koo-jes-se," who he recalled stating, "the men who built the ship and started with it all died—died with the Cold." Hall's journal entry continues:

> I asked him how he knew this? He said "all the old Innuits said so!" How will this agree with what the old Innuitt Woman, Mother of M-Garng said to me last winter in her oral history which she communicated to me. She says that the 5 men built a ship & started—but finding so much ice they could not proceed & finally froze to death!

When Hall returned home, he was invited to give several lectures. On November 11, 1862, the *Philadelphia Inquirer* reported on a recent lecture given by Hall to the Geographical and Statistical Society in New York: "The speaker dwelt at some length on the oral history obtained from the natives, and strange to say, he has been so careful in his notes as to write down any question propounded to them and their answers." Hall later published his account of his journey in 1865 and repeatedly refers to his interviews with local Inuit as "oral history." Hall's account of his interviewing practices as oral history occurs two years prior to Morrissey's Watson reference, and it more overtly describes interviewing as a core element in the practice of oral history.

Morrissey speculates that Allan Nevins may have sourced the term "oral history" from Joe Gould, a Harvard-educated local writer described as a Greenwich Village eccentric who widely proclaimed to anyone who would listen that he had been working on an epic nine-million-word book spanning hundreds of notebooks titled

An Oral History of Our Time based on conversations he had with everyday people. Gould was consistently seen writing this "oral history" in cheap notebooks. In a 1931 article in the *New Republic*, the poet and critic Horace Gregory stated: "For years, the adventures of Joe Gould have been a legend south of Fourteenth Street in New York City. To those who have not met him, Joe Gould, oral historian of our times, has assumed the dignity of a myth."

In 1942 Joseph Mitchell profiled Joe Gould in a classic *New Yorker* article titled "Professor Seagull": "Joe Gould is a jaunty and emaciated little man who has been a notable in the cafeterias, diners, barrooms, and dumps of Greenwich Village for a quarter of a century." Gould passed away in 1957 in a state-run psychiatric facility, and *An Oral History of Our Time* was never published. Mitchell revisited Gould in a second *New Yorker* profile, which led to the 1965 book *Joe Gould's Secret*, in which Mitchell asserted that Gould's "oral history" probably never really existed. Following publication, numerous eyewitness accounts emerged from individuals claiming to have seen the manuscript. In her book *Joe Gould's Teeth*, historian Jill Lepore wrote that the manuscript existed at one time and she speculates on the possibility of Gould's influence on Allan Nevins, positing that Nevins may have been one of the historians who received letters from Gould in 1931. "Chances are he wrote to Nevins and gave him the idea."

Joe Gould may have given Nevins the phrase "oral history," but historian Louie Starr wrote that Nevins first began thinking about institutionalized interviewing "for the benefit of future scholars" in 1931 while working on a biography of Grover Cleveland. In a 1963 oral history interview with Allan Nevins conducted by Frank Ernest Hill, the interviewer inquiries about Nevins's conceptualization of oral history:

> Q: It always has seemed to me, although I never said anything to you about it, that the idea for interviewing people had come from the work you and I did on the Rockefeller life. There was

one individual particularly whom we interviewed at great
length, and about three months after he died; you remarked at
the time, "well, we just got him in time!"

A: That's perfectly true. That was the former office boy in Standard
Oil offices. He had known Rockefeller from the time he himself
was sixteen years old or thereabouts. That was indeed aptly the
seed of Oral History. Then, too, I was well aware of the great
work that had been done by Hubert H. Bancroft in California in
interviewing old pioneers of the far west.

The modern oral history movement

The introduction and proliferation of mechanical audio recording
technologies—the wire recorder, followed by the reel-to-reel tape
recorder—completely transformed oral history in terms of practice
and purpose. The establishment of the oral history center at
Columbia University did, indeed, spark a cascading academic
movement in the United States that included the establishment of
the Regional Oral History Office at the University of California,
Berkeley, in 1953; the official establishment of the Oral History
Association in 1967; and by the early 1970s, the establishment of
oral history centers at UCLA, the University of Florida, the
University of California, Fullerton, the University of North Texas,
Baylor University, and the University of Kentucky. In 1965 there
were 89 identifiable oral history projects in the United States, and
by 1971, the number had grown to 230. However, this growth was
not limited to academia with projects being created by the Los
Angeles Psychoanalytical Society, the American Philosophical
Society in Philadelphia, and the Nebraska State Historical Society.

Although massively influential, the Columbia model at this time
was not an inclusive approach to documenting history, as it
primarily focused on elite and mostly white male individuals
whom Nevins characterized as those who had "lived significant
lives." By the 1960s, historical inquiry began to radically shift

perspective away from documenting and interpreting only the extraordinary elite and institutional experiences to seeking to understand the experiences of the ordinary people, a movement that was popularly framed as history from below. This intellectual trend occurred worldwide, with early influences from the French Annales School, which included the work of historians Mark Bloch, Fernand Braudel, Lucian Febvre, and British historian E. P. Thompson. These 1960s historians influenced a new generation of historians, many of whom turned to oral history practice to document and advocate for ordinary people's and marginalized groups' experiences, creating a more inclusive understanding of the past and challenging dominant historical narratives.

By the 1970s and early 1980s, oral history practice was being widely utilized by researchers across multiple disciplines in academia, as well as by community scholars and researchers outside of academia and in the public sector, with the primary goal of inserting individual stories into the historical record, but with a particular focus on documenting stories of non-elite and marginalized peoples. Increasingly, oral history projects focused on African Americans, women, immigrants, and the working class. In 1972 Alice and Staughton Lynd published *Rank and File*, an innovative book based on twenty-two interviews with working-class organizers documenting personal experiences back to the 1930s, emerging as an exemplary model for documenting labor history.

Folklorist and oral historian Lynwood Montell completed his dissertation on the Coe Ridge Negro Colony in Cumberland County, Kentucky, based on oral history interviews in 1964. Later published as *The Saga of Coe Ridge: A Study in Oral History*, Montell's interviews demonstrated the power of memory, oral history, and folklore in reconstructing everyday life in past communities. For her 1969 doctoral dissertation, folklorist

Gladys-Marie Fry conducted 150 oral history interviews for what would become her 1975 book, *Night Riders in Black Folk History*, which examined systemic racism in how white people exploited African Americans' fears of the supernatural. Feminist historian Sherna Gluck emerged as a leader of the contemporary oral history movement's trend toward amplifying marginalized groups in the 1970s and 1980s. In a 1999 reflection, Gluck remarked that her landmark article "What's So Special About Women? Women's Oral History" "meant not only interviewing 'non-elite'—in contrast to the first generation's heavy emphasis on the elite—but it meant exploring the personal." Gluck said, "It was not only who we interviewed, but the questions we asked that set us apart."

As oral history emerged as a global practice in the second half of the twentieth century, distinctly different approaches to oral history became more apparent. The Oral History Society in the United Kingdom makes a general characterization on its website: "Oral historians in Western Europe and North America have often focused on issues of identity and cultural difference, oral historians in Latin America and Eastern Europe have tended to pursue more overtly political projects." Projects can focus on conducting several interviews with several different people, versus the "life story approach" of conducting several interviews across multiple sessions with the same individuals. Large-scale interviewing initiatives that conduct short-form interviews, such as the BBC's Listening Project or StoryCorps in the United States, have pushed boundaries and tested definitions of oral history.

As the oral history movement rapidly grew, some traditional historians persisted in their distrust of memory and oral sources, leading to what historian Rebecca Sharpless termed a "prejudice against oral history that remained strong for more than fifty years." At the root of this distrust were the questions of reliability and trustworthiness of facts drawn from memory. In 1972 historian Barbara Tuchman criticized modern society's tendency toward "over-documentation" and the challenges it would pose to future historians. Tuchman specifically targets oral history: "With the appearance of the tape-recorder, a monster with the appetite of a tapeworm, we now have through its creature Oral History, an artificial survival of trivia of appalling proportions." In 1997 historian Eric Hobsbawm openly questioned personal memory's reliability, characterizing oral history as "a remarkably slippery medium for preserving facts." This diminishing (but enduring) distrust of oral history sources sparked a methodological and intellectual intensification by oral history scholars. In the 1997 publication of *The Death of Luigi Trastulli and Other Stories: Form and Meaning in Oral History*, Italian scholar Alessandro Portelli wrote:

> The discrepancy between fact and memory ultimately enhances the value of the oral sources as historical documents. It is not caused by faulty recollections...but actively and creatively generated by memory and imagination in an effort to make sense of crucial events and of history in general....Beyond the event as such, the real and significant historical fact which these narratives highlight is the memory itself.

Portelli's masterful exploration of a community's collective misremembering refocused the intellectual lens away from absolute and unquestioned factual truth, focusing on the cultural and historical value of the meaning of memory. In addition to Portelli, numerous historians, including Luisa Passerini, Ronald Grele, Michael Frisch, John Bodnar, Paul Thompson, Elizabeth Tonkin, and Alistair Thomson, have since comprehensively addressed oral history's memory and credibility question. Oral history's scholarly response acknowledged the narrative existence of bias, gaps in memory, and the human tendency toward exaggeration and nostalgia. However, oral historians' responses clearly revealed the very same characteristics were imbued throughout more traditional documentary primary sources.

Oral history projects now range from documentation of events, people, topics, and institutions to documenting crises, such as Columbia University's 9/11 oral history project, and activism and social justice. Today, the Oral History Association in the United States defines oral history as "a field of study and a method of gathering, preserving and interpreting the voices and memories of people, communities, and participants in past events." Although, over the years, there has been a shifting focus on documenting different communities for differing purposes, and different approaches emerged for interpreting and understanding interviews, the dominant contemporary definition of oral history has remained relatively constant. Contemporary oral history practice is generally perceived to be the recording, analysis, and preservation of knowledge created by the intentional act of an interviewer interviewing a person who possesses historical knowledge about a topic being documented or studied. Individually, an oral history interview is a personal exploration of experience and memory that provides a perspective rarely represented by traditional historical documentary sources.

As the definition of "oral history" broadened around the world in the first two decades of the twenty-first century, the core elements of this mainstream conceptualization of oral history practice persisted, rooted in interviewing, recording, preserving, and trying to best understand and interpret recorded life stories. However, in recent years it seems the dominant paradigm has been challenged in ways that return the core concepts of culture, community, and oral tradition back to the base definition of "oral history," especially within Indigenous communities. In the 2019 book *Rethinking Oral History and Tradition: An Indigenous Perspective*, New Zealand historian Nepia Mahuika writes:

> Oral history, for me, is very different from the popular "Western" academic conceptions that define it as a "democratic tool," a methodology based on the co-constructed interviews, life narratives,

and an interpretive mode of analysing stories captured via analog or digital recordings. Like those of many other indigenous thinkers, my interpretation rejects the idea that our oral histories must conform to the form and meanings popularized by non-indigenous academics, who tend to separate oral history and tradition as if they were two distinctively different fields. It defies a reading of our oral histories as false, unreliable, or the puerile imaginings of the "other." For us, oral history is not something to be found merely in a recorded interview, and while some have positioned native oral histories as "traditions," my indigenous understandings of oral history see them as more than chants, myths, and legends, and much more than merely an archive of interviews in a post-colonial era.

Similarly, Canadian oral historians Kristina R. Llewellyn, Alexander Freund, and Nolan Reilly take a broad view in defining oral history in their introduction to *The Canadian Oral History Reader*, where they acknowledge:

> Oral history has been practised for a long time, in different cultures and countries, and in many disciplines—from academic historians, sociologists, and ethnographers, to archivists, museum curators and other public historians, to journalists and activists. Defining oral history is therefore not easy; nor is it necessarily desirable, because any definition will exclude certain practices and practitioners.... definitions can easily be misunderstood or misused in an attempt to exclude.

Practitioners often create formal definitions when seeking clarity to professionalize and differentiate their practice from similar forms. In his 1998 article "Fifty Years On: An International Perspective on Oral History," historian Alistair Thomson explores earlier movements to narrow oral history interview techniques and "legitimize oral history by advocating a more 'scientific' model." This narrowing gave way to expansion as the interview later became viewed more as "a relationship embedded within particular cultural practices and informed by culturally specific systems and relations of communication." To underscore his point, Thomson references an interaction at an international oral history conference in 1994 when the Singaporean oral historian Daniel Chew "argued that the probing questions integral to a Western interview might not be appropriate or, indeed, possible in an Asian context where they could breach powerful cultural expectations about deference to the authority of elders." Just as there is not one way of conducting an oral history interview, the definition of "oral history" is also complex and culturally specific.

Oral history consists of oral narratives that recall, reflect on, commemorate, interpret, and attempt to understand the past. Built into this breakdown is the notion that an individual narrates historical stories; these narrations are transmitted from one person to others and are not performed in cultural, social, or historical isolation. Before historians wrote histories, remembered and narrated history was passed down through generations as spoken stories. History emerges from oral tradition, and knowledge of the past brings people together in the present by telling and retelling stories; sometimes, those stories are committed to the written word, but only sometimes. Oral history can be the intangible repertoire or corpus of community "stories" that have been remembered and passed down through the generations, but oral history can also be the tangible and more formal practice of recording an interview event between an interviewer and a narrator or interviewee. Typically, the phrase "oral history" implies something more than just a simple telling of a story; the phrase implies a story with intentionality and function. Some have said that "oral history is memory," but oral history is more than just a memory; it is a memory that is shared, and in the act of sharing, that memory, expressed in the form of a story, is then potentially preserved through time. The richness and complexity of oral history practice emerge from various methods and approaches for interviewing, recording, preserving, and ultimately understanding those stories.

Chapter 3
Asking questions: The oral history interview

Asking questions and telling stories is how we explore, discover, and learn; it is how we connect with and truly understand one another in the present, create friendships, and even fall in love. In some ways, we use stories to create, affirm, and reaffirm our personal and community identities. Stories are performed, often prompted by a question, stories are remembered, and sometimes, stories are repeated and passed down through generations. Although oral history mainly consists of stories, the oral history interview is not merely storytelling and passive listening. It is a complex combination of remembering and forgetting, narratives and silences, strategy and flexibility, humanity and technology, all of which are shaped by culture and tradition, underpinning individual biases and focused perspectives.

The interview is a research and documentary methodology utilized in various fields ranging from oral history to sociology, folklore, anthropology, and psychology. It is informed by the perspective of applications outside academia, such as journalism, market research, and even education and entertainment (for example, documentaries, podcasts, or talk shows), for purposes ranging from documentation and data gathering, research and analysis, and ultimately the generation of more comprehensive understandings of human perspectives and experiences. Interviews typically involve direct and purposeful verbal interaction between individuals who play discrete and essential roles in seeking and providing information. Broadly speaking, interviews contain a few definitional components, including purpose and structure, intentionality, and an inquiry-focused conversational flow that includes, among other elements, questions and answers. The interview is foundational to oral history practice; however, not all interviewing constitutes "oral history." So, what exactly constitutes an oral history interview?

The oral history interview

The oral history interview is a recorded event conducted between an interviewer and a narrator with personal experiential knowledge about historical understandings that the oral historian intends to understand better or document. Oral history–style interviewing focuses on documenting firsthand accounts, life histories, and the personal experiences of interviewees and narrators and narratively exploring and recording personal and community memories. In their important book *The Voice of the Past*, Paul Thompson and Joanna Bornat reflect that "there are many different styles of interviewing, ranging from the friendly, informal, conversational approach to the more formal, controlled style of questioning."

Although each oral history interviewer has their own style, and interviewing styles can change depending on the nature of the project, different types of interviews are utilized in oral history practice. Oral history interviews are considered by some academic disciplines, such as sociology, as "qualitative interviews." The oral history interview is not a random conversation; it has intention and purpose, and most often, an interview has a built-in topical structure. For example, many interviews are structured chronologically or topically, creating a loose "chapter" framework.

Even though most oral history interviews have a basic structure, oral history is considered a "semi-structured" interview. In a qualitative analysis framework, the "structured" interview tends to be more of a rigid survey, asking everyone the exact same questions. Oral history is considered "semi-structured" because, despite the topical structure or intended interview outline, the most important questions asked are those not in the interviewer's notes or outline. Often, these topical tangents or discussions are prompted by a follow-up question, followed by more follow-up questions.

There are multiple types of oral history projects, ranging from a community oral history to a biographical or life history project, from documenting experiences of people working in a particular industry or company to interviewing individuals who witnessed or participated in a specific event. A life history interview series can consist of three to four interview sessions but can also involve more than eighty sessions conducted with a single individual. For topical or event-style interviews, the interviewer may have just a single session with the narrator and must negotiate and balance the percentage of the interview that explores a more condensed or cropped version of their life history, potentially including personal memories or stories that are considered tangential or do not directly relate to the central topic or purpose of the interview. Most often, interviews have some perceived content focus; for example, an interview that is conducted for a project documenting activism during the civil rights movement in the United States in the 1960s would heavily focus on the topic of the narrator's experiences and memories as an activist.

However, context is essential to greater understanding, and sometimes, the seemingly tangential topics and details that emerge in an interview's cropped life history portion prove to be the most contextually useful and important information. It would be a mistake to launch an oral history interview conducted with an activist by asking the initial question, "Can you tell me about your first memories of activism?" What you lose by immediately launching into the narrator's activism can be the rich life experiences that contextualize and frame their activism later in life. Still, the interviewer may have only a single session to interview this individual, and thus will have to proactively manage the interview agenda and balance and prioritize the discussion of contextually rich, albeit tangential elements of life history with interview content more directly related to the oral history project's core or central topic. Nonetheless, it is often the content discussed during a topical interview's preliminary life history section that prompts magical connections made later in the interview.

While oral history interviewing tends not to be completely unstructured, there is a more ethnographic approach to interviews featuring more guided conversations conducted over multiple sessions. Traditional ethnography is rooted in anthropology and folklore practice and typically involves a more immersive study of people, communities, and cultures. It also consists of a participant or embedded observational focus over time. The ethnographic style of oral history interviewing involves deeply engaging with narrators' cultural, social, and personal contexts. It focuses on interpreting life stories in the broader framework of community and identity. An exemplary example of the more ethnographic approach to oral history fieldwork would be the dialogic approach of the Italian oral historian Alessandro Portelli, who conducted interviews over two decades in the same community in eastern Kentucky. His work culminated in the book *They Say in Harlan County: An Oral History*. This interviewing style is akin to the ethnographic fieldwork approaches of folklorists like Henry Glassie and his work in the model ethnography *Passing the Time in Ballymenone: Culture and History of an Ulster Community*, drawn from multiple years of fieldwork documenting a Northern Irish community. This approach has a significantly heavier emphasis on relationship building and engagement over extended periods of time. In a lecture delivered at the University of Kentucky in 2010, Portelli reflected on his interviewing experiences conducted in Harlan County:

> I didn't come to teach anything; I came to learn. And this was a lesson in the methodology of fieldwork of oral history that has lasted all my life since then...the only reason you're doing the interview is because that person knows things that you don't know. You're there to learn. You're not there to confirm previous knowledge.

By nature, oral history interviews tend to be open-ended and have a flow. Typically, an individual oral history interview is, thematically, part of a larger project, or there is a particular point of emphasis or a topical focal point creating a loose structure to the session. However, there is a built-in flexibility to the oral history interview that frees the participants to explore unintended topics serendipitously throughout an interview. The oral history interview is far more than a story-gathering exercise conducted by the story collector.

Sharing authority

There are two roles played in the oral history interview experience: the interviewer who asks questions, asks follow-up questions, decides when not to ask questions, and changes the topics as they guide the overall trajectory of an interview to fit the aim of the oral history project, and the narrator, who responds to the questions and the framing of the interview, telling stories that are sometimes deeply personal and articulating memories. Traditionally, there was a sense in oral history practice that the interviewer, the oral historian, or the primary researcher with a specific intention was the authority in the interviewer–narrator relationship. However, in 1990, historian Michael Frisch published *A Shared Authority: Essays on the Craft and Meaning of Oral and Public History* and introduced the democratizing concept of collaboratively sharing this authority with the narrators in the history-making process.

The introduction of this concept sparked a movement within oral history to think more collaboratively about the interview process and perceive it more as a creative partnership. This change in perception and, eventually, in practice, reframed the dialogic relationship of an interview into co-authorship. The notions of reflexivity, transparency, and reciprocity are important when sharing authority in an interview context. An interviewer must reflect on their role in this process and co-construct an empowering interview for all participants. The concept of sharing authority introduced a significant dimension to interviewing practice, challenging the traditional perceptions of the primacy of the interviewer or historian over the narrator and their community. The interview is a co-created and collaborative session involving what Alessandro Portelli calls a "deep exchange" between multiple authors in multiple voices.

Interviewing and intersubjectivity

Alessandro Portelli explores numerous aspects and angles of oral history interviewing in his influential book *The Battle of Valle Giulia: Oral History and the Art of Dialogue*. In addition to this notion of an interview as a deep exchange, Portelli explores the uniqueness and originality of the interview session. Although the narrator may have told some of these stories many times before, Portelli posits, "What is spoken in a typical oral history interview has usually never been told *in that form* before." Even if an interviewer asks multiple individuals the same questions across an oral history project, and even if a narrator has told a story hundreds of times before, an oral history interview between two individuals may create something distinctive and unique. Indeed, the focus of the interview is on the narrator's individual life story, lived experiences, and personal memories; however, both participants—the interviewer and the person being interviewed—bring their personal worldviews, agendas, subjectivities, personal baggage, and even biases into the interview event. From the moment the recorder is turned on and the first question is asked, there is an interweaving of individuals, their ideas, and their perspectives, resulting in an intersubjectivity that results in unique and meaningful dialogue.

Intersubjectivity in an oral history context refers to the mutual influence between individuals engaged in dialogue. The oral history interview is a collaborative process in which the interviewer and interviewee co-create a narrative based on memory and past experiences. As expected, this dynamic completely varies depending on who is asking and who is answering the questions. A successful oral history interview relies on the openness of the narrator to share personal stories and memories, often infused with emotion and identity. Success also depends on the interviewer's self-awareness of what they bring to the interview—their insider/outsider status, agendas, and biases.

When looking at an oral history interview through the lens of intersubjectivity, one can critically and appropriately acknowledge the power differentials inherent in oral history interviews. The interviewer typically occupies a perceived position of authority; the interviewer makes the foundational decisions on which themes the interview will explore, and the interviewer, by definition, will steer the conversation. However, intersubjectivity denotes a dynamic of mutual influence, where the narrator can and will assert agency, selecting which stories to tell, emphasizing particular memories, or ultimately redirecting (or derailing) the interview and resulting narrative.

A "peculiar" practice

An oral history interview is not just a recorded session where an inquiring historian asks good questions. So much is simultaneously unfolding in real time below the surface of the conversation. In his book *The Death of Luigi Trastulli and Other*

Stories: Form and Meaning in Oral History, Portelli makes the case for oral history as a distinctive genre of historical practice. He identifies six elements that make interviews "intrinsically different" from other primary sources: the orality of oral sources, oral history as narrative, meaning and subjectivity, credibility, objectivity, and co-authorship.

An oral history interview is not just a recorded session where an inquiring historian asks good questions. So much of oral history is rooted in the spoken word. Unlike written records or images, the orality of oral history interviews preserves nuanced speech patterns, intonations and inflections, pauses, sarcasm, and emotions. The interview's orality underscores the interview's immediacy and implies a mutually exchanged performance. Ultimately, the oral history interview is structured narratively and shaped by the participants' intersubjectivities. Interviewers pose questions, and memories are imagined, reframed, and articulated in stories infused with the narrator's subjectivities.

Despite oral historians' efforts to establish oral history as a credible primary source, Portelli argues that the assumption of factual accuracy (or lack thereof) does not provide credibility to oral history. Sometimes, misremembering and expressing factual inaccuracies can have significant meanings that reflect deeply held beliefs, trauma, culture, and the resonance of collective or community memories. Finally, through his framing of objectivity and authorship, Portelli embraces oral history's intersubjective and collaborative nature.

In her book *Oral History Theory*, historian Lynn Abrams presents the concept of intersubjectivity as a "collision" between the two subjectivities of interviewer and interviewee. Abrams continues: "More than that, it describes how the subjectivity of each is shaped by the encounter with the other." Fundamentally, oral history theory and practice come down to the dynamic complexities underlying the recorded interview. Yet it is still about asking good questions, creating a strong rapport with those we are interviewing, empowering people, and collaboratively expanding the historical narrative.

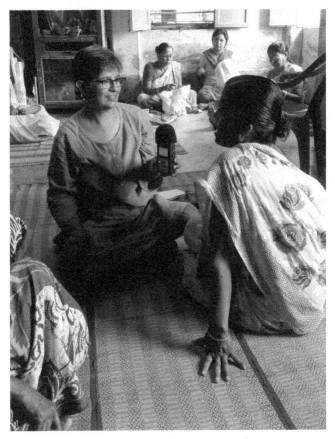

3. Indira Chowdhury interviews Dipali Pramanik at Kolaghat Mahila Samiti, Kolaghat, West Bengal, for the Sasha Association for Craft Producers, 2015.

Feminist oral history

Feminist theory profoundly influenced oral history theory and methodology. In her 1977 article "What's So Special About Women? Women's Oral History," feminist historian Sherna Gluck advocated for oral history's role in challenging the "traditional concepts of history" and "affirming that our everyday lives are history." Gluck, former director of the California State University, Long Beach Oral History Program, advocated for a more inclusive historical record and the centering of women's voices and experiences.

Feminist interviewing methodology places particular emphasis on power differentials, subjectivity, and reflexivity, a collaborative approach to interviewing, and an openness to exploring a wider range of topics that include the everyday experiences of women. Feminist oral history profoundly influenced the ethical standards of oral history and generated a greater mindfulness toward the interview dynamic. In their article "Learning to Listen: Interview Techniques and Analysis," Kathryn Anderson and Dana C. Jack elaborate on the methodological implications of feminist oral history:

> Women's oral history requires much more than a new set of questions to explore women's unique experiences and unique perspectives; we need to refine our methods for probing more deeply by listening to the levels on which the narrator responds to the original questions. To do so we need to listen critically to our interviews, to our responses as well as to our questions. We need to hear what women implied, suggested, and started to say but didn't. We need to interpret their pauses and, when it happens, their unwillingness or inability to respond. We need to consider carefully whether our interviews create a context in which women feel comfortable exploring the subjective feelings that give meaning to actions, things, and events, whether they allow women to explore "un-womanly" feelings and behaviors, and whether they encourage women to explain what they mean in their own terms.

Oral history and journalistic interviewing

For most people, the basic concept of an "interview" is typically associated with journalism. Most news stories, whether written or broadcast, normally contain direct quotations from someone relevant to the story. Elicited by a direct conversation between the journalist and the eyewitness, these quotations effectively emphasize the point in the journalist's story.

Today's online journalism requires a greater emphasis on search engine optimization. Since the beginning of this century, journalism—especially news stories involving popular culture—has embraced the phrase "oral history" as a title convention for any news story derived from an interview about anything in the past, especially in the United States. A quick Google News search of "oral history" will produce titles such as "Radiohead's 'OK Computer': An Oral History" and "Pure Magic: The Oral History of Prince's Super Bowl XLI Halftime Show." And the trend is prevalent in politics as well: "Covering Trump: An Oral History of an Unforgettable Campaign" or "Election Day 2016 Oral History—What Really Happened on Election Day." It is as if "oral history" is used in titles by the publications to strengthen the stories' gravitas or historical impact or to evoke nostalgia, both of which intend to tempt the reader or listener into clicking on the story.

If both journalistic and oral history interviews can focus on the individual perspective and be historical in nature, what is it that differentiates these two forms of interviewing? In 2004 Mark Feldstein, a media and public affairs professor and a long-time broadcast journalist, examined the similarities, differences, and relationships. He concludes:

> Journalism and oral history are both related and separate. Their reliance on interviews leads to similar if not identical techniques; their interactions with human subjects raise similar issues of

empathy and ethics. Yet the two disciplines operate in different spheres of time and ultimately have different ends.

Journalistic interviewing is often about creating an immediate outcome in the form of an article or a story that is probably driven by a deadline. Both oral history and journalistic interviews are driven by the hope of obtaining greater understanding and meaning; however, journalistic interviews are often more greatly focused on hyper-specific topics, and they are less tolerant of topical digressions that may or may not result in contextual connections. The "life history" details and the personal memories encouraged over the course of an oral history interview, whether directly relevant or not to the interview or project core, are invaluable components of what constitutes an oral history interview. The journalistic interview tends to be more directly functional in purpose and outcome. In 2009 the Oral History Association in the United States differentiated oral history interviewing in its *Principles and Best Practices*:

> Oral history is distinguished from other forms of interviews by its content and extent. Oral history interviews seek an in-depth account of personal experience and reflections, with sufficient time allowed for the narrators to give their story the fullness they desire. The content of oral history interviews is grounded in reflections on the past as opposed to commentary on purely contemporary events.

When considering the differences between oral history and journalistic interviewing, one must tread carefully to avoid sweeping generalizations. Some journalists conduct very effective oral history–style interviews, just as there are oral historians conducting superficial, micro-focused, twenty-minute interviews that are recorded and archived as oral history. That said, the greatest distinction between journalistic and oral history interviews is in the purpose. Although most oral history interviews are conducted for a specific purpose or outcome, such as an academic article, a book, a podcast, or a documentary, unlike the journalistic cousin, oral history interviews are conducted under the assumption by both interviewer and narrator that the raw interview recording and/or transcript of such will be eventually made publicly available in its original form. In oral history, the interview is the primary source, whereas in journalism, the interview is used and quoted to create a distinct secondary resource, and journalism's raw interviews are rarely preserved and rarely accessed by anyone else but the interviewer. The functional approach to interviewing in a journalistic context results in an inherently more extractive model that rarely yields a level of detail and emotion at the same scale as an oral history interview.

Interviewees in a journalistic context tend to be viewed as "sources" of information, providing stories that contribute to the journalist's final work. Oral history interviewing prioritizes a sense of shared authority, collaboration, and co-creation of the recorded interview and the oral history project. The typical journalistic style of interviewing tends to privilege the journalist's authority, while the typical oral history style of interviewing privileges the narrator or interviewee's authority. Although both approaches utilize inquiry in the form of interviewing, there tends to be distinct philosophical and practical differences between the journalistic and the oral history interview.

An effective oral history interview

Many resources will tell you what constitutes "best practice" for conducting a good oral history interview. There are books and handbooks such as Donald A. Ritchie's classic *Doing Oral History*; Beth M. Robertson's *Oral History Handbook*, published by the Oral History Australia; *The Routledge Guide to Interviewing: Oral History, Social Enquiry and Investigation* by Anna Bryson and Sean McConville; or *Memories & Reflections: The Singapore Experience*, published by the National Archives of Singapore. There are numerous in-person and synchronous streaming workshops hosted by various institutions, including Baylor

University's Institute for Oral History and the Oral History Summer Institute hosted by the Columbia Center for Oral History Research at Columbia University. Many national professional organizations, including Oral History Australia (OHA), the Oral History Society in the United Kingdom, and the Oral History Association in the United States, regularly hold introductory, practical, and interactive workshops on interviewing methodology. Essentially, most of these resources boil down to some fundamental approaches. Interviewing is more of an art than it is a science; I do not like to think of myself as an interviewer "conducting" oral interviews, as much as I like to think of it as collaborating to create an oral history interview.

Conducting preliminary research

No matter how informed, accomplished, or brilliant the interviewer may be, it is essential to conduct thorough research before an interview for any interviewer to be most effective. Research conducted prior to each interview will provide a level of depth and breadth necessary for asking good questions, and it will also demonstrate your level of commitment to the interview and to the project. It is necessary to have a strong knowledge of historical contexts at the community, regional, national, and international levels, but it is also vitally important to have a sense of the personal historical context. Yes, conducting research will help to create a useful outline or list of questions; however, more importantly, it will enable the interviewer to ask more effective follow-up questions. Pre-interview research is essential to composing and framing questions; however, an interviewer must first identify and understand the historical and cultural contexts of the narrator and the potential thematic or topical trajectory of their story to conduct an effective and meaningful interview. Simply asking open-ended questions and "winging it" will not typically yield substantive results.

Beginning the interview

There are two essential elements for beginning oral history interviews. First, the interviewer should conduct an introductory conversation (before recording commences) about the oral history project and the narrator's specific role in the project and provide a comprehensive frame for the narrator's informed consent to participate. Unless they are public figures, most narrators do not fully understand why you are talking to them, or they do not feel that they are historically important enough to be featured.

Second, beginning each interview with a formal introductory statement is important. For example, include in the statement your name, the date, the name of the person you are interviewing, the oral history project name, and the sponsoring institution or archival repository. This formal introduction has numerous important functions. An interviewer will probably have conversations with their narrator upon arrival and during the setup phase of the interview. This preliminary conversation can often drift into the realm of topics the interviewer wants to discuss in the interview. Small talk-style conversation before the interview can be extremely useful to deflect the narrator from conversations an interviewer wants to save for the interview. The formal introduction will create a strong transition from casual conversation and frame the interview that is about to begin. Additionally, this formality conveys that this interview is valued and important to the interviewer and the institution preserving the interview.

Finally, this formal introduction serves as the ultimate identifying metadata. On the archival side, imprinting this identifying information onto the recording will prove invaluable. Archives that have been practicing oral history through the years are probably familiar with adhesive labels falling off audiocassette tapes, leaving recordings unidentified. The digital equivalent is the transmission to the archive of a digital file with an unidentifiable file name that has not been changed to reflect the participants or the projects. On its own, the archive would turn to the recording to identify the participants of an interview and associate that interview with a particular oral history project or archival collection.

The first question

Once the interview formally begins, it is helpful to test the waters, so to speak, and begin with an open-ended question. If interviewing someone for the first time, it is useful to start with something like: "Tell me a little about yourself." This question is open-ended and is a question the narrator cannot get wrong. This helps to assuage any fear or insecurities they may have coming into the interview. The interviewer will often notice visible relief on the narrator's face when posing this initial question. There is a built-in power imbalance in the oral history interview on multiple levels, but one example is the narrator's anticipatory anxiety from ambiguity about what will be discussed in the interview. In advance of the interview, the narrator typically does not know what questions will be asked and the interviewer is selectively guiding the topics and choosing which questions and topics to follow up on. Beginning the interview with "Tell me a little about yourself" empowers the narrator to set the initial tone and choose the details and stories they will use to introduce themselves. In addition, starting with this question provides useful details and clues for the interviewer regarding the narrator's expression of self and identity. Often, the interviewer can utilize small details gleaned from the opening answer to this first question to create better contextual understandings later in the interview.

The second question

If beginning the interview with "Tell me a little about yourself," the second question is just as important. After the narrator concludes their answer to the first question, a suggested second question will always be a follow-up question directly associated with something the narrator said during their answer to the opening question. An interviewer could approach these two questions like a mental game, forcing themselves to intensely focus on what is said in answer to "Tell me a little about yourself" and generate a relevant follow-up question relating to the narrator's initial answer. Functionally, this approach sends the initial framing message that the interviewer will listen closely and ask relevant questions, but it also functions to indicate to the narrator that the interviewer values their story. This approach is very effective at quickly and efficiently building rapport with a narrator.

Building rapport

No matter what stories the narrator tells and what topics an interviewer ignores from a content standpoint, an interviewer will conduct an effective oral history interview if able to successfully connect on some level with the narrator. Most of the time, an interviewer will interview individuals they do not already know well, unless they are interviewing for a project documenting one's own family or community. Creating and maintaining rapport in such a brief encounter can be a challenge, but it is important to intentionally make a positive connection with your narrator. It is impossible to underscore enough the importance of doing one's homework prior to the interview session and being prepared with background information, historical context, and a thoughtful outline or list of questions. If the interviewer is unprepared, the narrator will pick up on that immediately and feel disrespected, setting a negative tone for the entire interview. However, if the interviewer is well prepared, the narrator will be flattered and comfortable. Additionally, it is important to conduct the interview in a comfortable setting, if possible. The kitchen table, especially over a cup of tea or coffee, is a comfortable place for conversation and connection.

One of the most important aspects of creating a connection and building rapport is actively listening to the narrator. Active listening can contain numerous elements, but ultimately it comes down to the interviewer demonstrating interest and engagement. Occasional and strategic verbal affirmations such as "That is interesting," or even an occasional "Hmmm," accompanied by a nod of the head, are all that is needed. But these should be occasional and strategic because being too "active" is possible. Constantly interrupting with verbal affirmations could potentially be off-putting, distracting, and uncomfortable to the narrator. Give the narrator the space to speak, but actively demonstrate that you are engaged through nods of the head and occasional verbal affirmations, as well as maintaining eye contact throughout the interview. Finally, connect through the way you ask questions or in your responses. Do not avoid empathy or hesitate to show emotion. In fact, the opposite is best: be empathetic and show emotion throughout the interview process. The oral history interview is intimate and connective by nature. I have interviewed numerous individuals who hold strongly expressed views and beliefs I may disagree with, yet in most cases, the oral history interview creates a connection point that can last long beyond the interview.

Asking good questions

Although the content of a question is important to effective interviewing, how one asks the question can be equally important. One of the reasons why the "Tell me a little about yourself" question is such a good first question in an interview is the fact that it is open-ended. An open-ended question allows space for the interviewee to shape their answers without undue influence. There is a reason "leading the witness" is a common objection when questioning someone testifying in a court of law. An unidentified interview archived at the Kentucky Historical Society demonstrates the influence of leading questions.

INTERVIEWER: What would you say between those days and the days we live in now, were they more peaceful and were you more at ease in your early days than the public is today?

NARRATOR: Sure, more at ease, more ease.

INTERVIEWER: Would you say that life was easier?

NARRATOR: Life was easier. Life was easier and say there's a few people and we had no trouble with one another.

This is a clear example of the impact of asking leading questions. How an interviewer asks questions will affect the answer, which is why asking open-ended questions is critically important. A better way to ask the question would be, "Could you describe for me your memories of life back then?" and following up as needed.

In addition to asking well-formed questions, it is important to consider the timing of questions. Some interviewers take the collaborative aspects of the oral history interview to the extreme and continuously interrupt and interject their own perspectives. For example, in March 1994 Colonel Arthur Kelly, for the Nunn Center's American Veterans: World War Two Oral History Project, interviewed Ralph Devine of Springfield, Kentucky, who served as a medic in the US Army. The narrator is speaking about approaching Utah Beach on D-Day and how the landing craft he was on turned over on its side when it hit the beach:

KELLY: And then was it pretty well packed with the forty men or so?

DEVINE: Well, yes.

KELLY: Now, when it turned over, where were you?

DEVINE: I was towards the rear end.

KELLY: And did they…

DEVINE: Just dumped us out.

KELLY: Into the water?

DEVINE: No, really wasn't… we was out of the water.

KELLY: Were you?

DEVINE: Umhmm. Oh, we got wet and nasty, but…

KELLY: Muddy or…

DEVINE: Yeah, muddy. Real muddy.

KELLY: You said something about mud. So you were dumped into the mud.

DEVINE: Yes, sir.

KELLY: People fall on top of you or...

DEVINE: Yes, sir. And it was the awfullest scramble you ever seen. Everybody was like me, they was scared to death.

KELLY: Well, tell me about that. Tell me what happened. Describe to me...were you standing at the moment...

DEVINE: Yes, we were all...we were all standing.

KELLY: And you were toward the rear?

DEVINE: And I was toward the rear.

The interviewer's continual interruption clearly prevents the narrator from elaborating on any point and greatly impacts the interview dynamic and the resulting interview content.

The interview's content core

There are specific reasons certain people are asked and selected to participate in an oral history project. Ralph Devine was chosen to be interviewed for the Nunn Center's American Veterans: World War Two Oral History Project because he was, indeed, a World War II veteran. Likewise, Beulah Collins was selected by historian Charles Hardy to be interviewed for the *Goin' North: Stories from the First Great Migration to Philadelphia*, documenting the African American experience because Beulah Collins migrated to Philadelphia in 1919 after her husband died of influenza during the 1918 pandemic. In both cases, there is an obvious "core topic" focus for each interview. When talking about the importance of documenting "life history," even in the case of a single interview, interviewers must continuously balance the need for context with the choices of what topics will get the primary focus during the interview. In the case of Beulah Collins, the primary topical focal points of the *Goin' North* project involved documenting memories not only of the migration to Philadelphia but also their lives in Philadelphia since migration. The interview's index reveals the interview structure with the following "chapter points" or segment titles:

00:00:02 – Hometown of Snow Hill, Maryland: Life on the farm

00:05:43 – Moving to Philadelphia, circa 1919

00:09:16 – Domestic service: Living with the Richard family in Philadelphia

00:11:32 – On boarding her son with "Mom" Taylor

00:17:46 – Domestic service in Philadelphia

00:20:59 – Domestic service: Low wages

00:27:11 – Domestic service: Long hours

00:33:18 – Work options as a Black woman in Philadelphia

00:36:07 – Memories of the South and her husband's death in 1918

00:41:49 – Memories of her childhood as a tenant farmer's daughter

00:44:21 – Final thoughts: Religious leaders and the Great Depression

The interviewer, Charles Hardy, skillfully documents important aspects of Collins's life in Maryland before she migrated to Philadelphia but moves into the interview's core topics very efficiently. Hardy made the decision not to delve too deeply into Collins's family history, beginning the interview by briefly exploring Collins's childhood on the farm but asking the questions "When did you come up to Philadelphia? When did you come North?" just prior to the six-minute mark in the interview. Hardy could have spent an entire hour just discussing Collins's childhood and family history, but within six minutes Collins was into adulthood, discussing her marriage in 1917. The specific point of the oral history project and this interview was to document the personal experience of migration and her life as an African American in Philadelphia. In this case, the interviewer made an important choice to introduce the interview's core topic early in the interview. While this is not always the case, it is important to be mindful of the core topics of an interview, anticipate what topics outside of the core are necessary and likely, and build the interview around those core topics.

Embrace digression

In the Beulah Collins interview, Hardy moves through some topics efficiently, such as Collins's childhood, but chooses to elaborate on other topics, such as Collins's work in domestic service for a white family in Philadelphia's Chestnut Hill neighborhood. Initially, there is a clean sequential structure to the interview until near the thirty-eight-minute mark when Hardy asks, "How did life in Philadelphia compare to your life in Maryland?" This breaks the memory and story sequence and returns to the topic of growing up on the farm. Collins proceeds to reflect on life before Philadelphia:

> COLLINS: ... I didn't want to go back and live down on the farm and raise chickens and cows and things now. Of course, I'm older, but I never did after I come up and got up here and got working, I never went back there. I never cared to go back there. We had, uh, people down there and widows down there. I could have gone down there and stayed, but I didn't want to. I wanted to stay up here where my baby could have a better education. I was living for him. That was my idea because he had no father, his father was dead. And his father and I was the cause of him being here and I felt it was my duty to take care of him.

A skillful interviewer, Hardy recognized the value of this topical digression and embraced it, filling in some of the gaps left by such a quick transition to adulthood and migration at the beginning of the interview. Recognizing the importance of improvisation and recognizing when to follow potential digressions is an important skill that will lead to rich discussion and important memories that the interviewer may not have anticipated.

Asking good questions

Oral historian Charles Morrissey advocates for the value of the use of a two-part question for framing follow-up questions: "it continually affirms essential elements in the relationship between interviewer and interviewee as co-creators of an oral history document—the questions and answers that constitute the product of this joint endeavor." Essentially, this approach involves the interviewer drawing on content from preliminary research or content already discussed in the interview and synthesizing that information to set up the next question.

The following example of the two-sentence structuring of questions comes from an interviewer, Tanya Pearson, who posed a series of two-sentence style questions to Scottish musician Shirley Manson from Pearson's Women of Rock Oral History Project. At this point in the interview, Manson reflected on her experience acting in the television series *Terminator: The Sarah Connor Chronicles*. As the interviewer, Pearson, transitions to the next topic, she sets up the next question by making a specific reference to a musical shift in tone that occurred between Manson's band Garbage's release of the album *Not Your Kind of People* and the album *Strange Little Birds*:

> PEARSON: Getting back together, *Not Your Kind of People* was like a reaction to being rejected by labels and you're doing everything yourself. *Strange Little Birds*, I love....*Not Your Kind of People* seemed kind of more political, and you seemed pissed off. *Strange Little Birds*, I was really surprised lyrically because you seemed to really be expressing the insecurities that you said you've had since you were young, which I never would have guessed.

Without Pearson needing to articulate part two of the two-sentence structure (the actual question), the narrator proceeds:

> MANSON: Well, it's interesting that you talk about the *Terminator* experience.... My agent said to me, "Look, if you want to do any more acting, you're going to need to study with a teacher."... And so eventually I garnered the confidence and the balls to walk into an acting class. And I was so lucky that I stumbled upon this incredible teacher called Sharon Chatten. And while studying under this woman, she taught me a couple of really incredible fundamental things that have really stuck with me about being an artist, about telling the truth, about how you can only really be your best, most complete self as an artist when you're telling hundred percent the truth and you're not serving anything but your own story.... It changed something in me. And I realized that the stakes were getting higher and higher for me as a woman. I was aging. You know, when we made *Strange Little Birds*, I was coming up to being fifty. And I suddenly realized that I had been in service a lot of my career to what people expected from me, what people wanted from me.... And when I came into *Strange Little Birds*, I guess I just felt selfish and thought, "You know, your time, literally, your time is running out. And why don't you just try and be brave and actually be your authentic self?"

Pearson's thoughtful and compelling question setup prompts rich content and reflective elaboration. Although it seems simplistic, the two-sentence question format powerfully demonstrates the collaborative, shared, and co-authoring aspects of oral history interviewing. By directly referencing specific albums and songs, and her observed difference in tones between albums, Pearson overtly demonstrates the value of conducting comprehensive preliminary research for enabling specific and informed questions.

4. Tanya Pearson interviews Shirley Manson for the Women of Rock Oral History Project, 2018.

Finally, Pearson personalizes her question by reflecting on her own surprise that Manson struggled with insecurity. Once more, Pearson did not need to complete part two of her question before Manson proceeded:

PEARSON: Yeah, when I played it, "Sometimes," it's the first song.... I could identify with so much of the lyrical content on the album. And I was just like, "Oh man, she had the guts to say it, to just," it seemed like you were singing...just like a journal entry.

MANSON: Yeah, it was that kind of raw. And that's rough to do...but it felt exciting, felt dangerous to me. And I guess I just want...I want excitement now when I'm in the studio. I don't want to be writing a pop song that a twenty-year-old could sing. I'm like, "What is the most valuable artist I can be?" It's telling the truth about what it means to have lived my kind of life, my career, at fifty-one...women aren't supposed to age and we're not supposed to be seen past thirty. So, I felt it was a somewhat punk rock act.

By posing conversational questions rooted in nuanced knowledge, Pearson signals this is not just another celebrity interview and creates a reflective opportunity for Manson. Good questions, even when the actual question is implied, will often elicit and inspire profound answers.

The reflective turn and creating meaning

The following are goals for an oral history interviewer conducting an interview: Ask good questions; find relevance; ask follow-up questions; make connections; ask more questions; and create meaning and understanding. Throughout an interview, there will be times when the flow of the interview will focus largely on description, but there will be opportunities throughout an interview to take a reflective and illuminating turn and follow a path of inquiry designed to create deeper connections and come to new understandings. The question tree metaphor is useful when considering interviewing technique. Question branches will typically begin as descriptive. As the branch extends out and the topic begins to weaken, consider a reflective turn, which potentially begins a new branch. Recognize the appropriateness or the effectiveness of that reflective turn and consider when the time is right to return to the trunk of the interview tree and start a new line of questioning.

It can also be useful to use the "funnel" approach to asking questions, where the interviewer begins broadly and progressively narrows in focus and specificity as the line of questioning progresses. But ultimately, the goal for any interview is to find the four-leaf clovers. In the sequence of asking questions, finding relevance, making connections, and creating meaning and understanding, the four-leaf clovers in interviews are those rare moments when an interviewer can use questions to create a transformative moment.

In 2013 I interviewed the actor Steve Zahn about a recent trip he had taken to interact with military troops stationed in Iraq in a USO-style visit. I had known from previous conversations over coffee with Zahn that he had a lifelong fascination with the military. We were conducting interviews with the veterans returning from the recent wars in Iraq and Afghanistan, and I thought it would be interesting to document a different angle of military life, specifically his experience of being tasked with boosting troop morale.

Even though the interview's core topic was Zahn's trip to Iraq, I chose to ask about life growing up in Minnesota, where he reflected on his fascination with the military, his love for military films growing up, and, like many other children, often pretending to be a soldier. He told a specific story about when he was a child, pretending to be in the Battle of the Bulge, digging a trench, and sitting outside in the Minnesota winter. Near the seven-minute mark, Zahn reflected on his fascination with the military: "For me, it was an emotional connection, which is interesting that I—my life went into acting and pretending." Once more, despite the interview's core topic, I felt compelled to ask this accomplished actor about some of his early acting experiences. We discussed his journey to becoming a professional actor, beginning his film career with *Reality Bites*. Very quickly, the conversation turned to some of the military films, such as *Rescue Dawn*, and how he had hoped for a role acting in *Saving Private Ryan* but was unsuccessful.

At about the twenty-eight-minute point in the interview, we transitioned to the topic of his trip to Iraq. Zahn described being prepared for the trip, the journey overseas, and the other participants in that particular trip.

> ZAHN: It was very strange. And then we got on Blackhawks. I remember in the morning, we're waiting for them to come in. You always waited for them; they didn't wait for you. You know, it was a different deal. And...the guys came out, and they gave us kind of the safety—which was like if we go down, you get away from the chopper. We're going to meet at the back of the chopper. There's weapons. It was just crazy. Like, okay, this is more than just—this is how you buckle your seatbelt. Can you run the emergency? It was different. Everything was different. We got on the Blackhawks and took off. And, um, loud, low. I remember just looking out and seeing camels and just desert and the other Blackhawk with the other half of our crew and just being floored. And then them coming over and saying like "We're in Iraq."

Throughout every oral history interview, an interviewer makes dozens of split-second decisions about how to proceed. At that moment, drawing on our previous discussions of Zahn playing pretend as a child and acting in military films earlier in his career, I posed the question: "Did you have a moment on that flight, just thinking back again from what we've talked about, where you realized this wasn't pretend?" Examining this moment in the interview video recording, the actor's physical reaction to my question, the look on his face, his reflective pause and tone of voice, and his change in posture, followed by placing both hands behind his head and slightly arching his back, all indicated that he was not expecting that question and had not thought about that moment from that perspective before. Zahn responded, "Yes. Yes, totally. I mean I—yeah, it was really—this was a real deal." After a slight pause, Zahn regrouped, and the interview flow resumed. Reflecting on the interview experience, this was clearly a breakthrough moment of "deep exchange," a moment when the interviewer and narrator, together, navigate questions, tell stories followed by more questions, find relevance, and create new meanings and understandings. Moments like this are special, rare, and important. Interviewers will not experience these moments in every interview they conduct, but when they do, the interviews are transformed. I walk into every interview with this goal in mind. The Steve Zahn interview was elevated by that moment, by that single follow-up question.

After that interview concluded, we took a picture together (because he is famous), and I walked Steve to the door, at which time he paused, turned, and remarked, "I've done a lot of films over the years, but when I am gone, this interview is what I want my children and grandchildren to watch." When conducting oral history interviews, an interviewer will spend most of the time exploring descriptions and recollections, but it is important to recognize and seek out the rare, transforming, and illuminating moments, seek out the creation of new meanings and understandings, and aspire for connection.

Chapter 4
Designing an oral history project

In our present moment, it is difficult to imagine a world in which the notion of voice recording was novel and once unimaginable, but that was the case when, in 1957, Hazel de Berg first brought home a reel-to-reel tape recorder. De Berg was a trained x-ray technician, a photographer, and a mother of three children living in the eastern suburbs of Sydney, Australia. She had initially acquired the tape recorder to launch a project to record books for people who were blind or sight-impaired. De Berg's daughter recalled, "In Mum's words, 'I wanted to read Mary Gilmore's *Old Days, Old Ways* and thought—since I knew Dame Mary—it might be a good idea to get her to say why she wrote it.'" Over the next twenty-seven years, de Berg conducted 1,290 recorded interviews with authors and poets and would later expand her project to interviewing Australians from a variety of backgrounds, including artists (musicians, painters, potters, sculptors, and actors) as well as journalists, broadcasters, librarians, politicians, judges, and scientists, to name just a few categories. De Berg extensively documented the experiences of women; local, regional, and national histories; and the topics of education, healthcare, and folklore.

In 1960 de Berg received a grant of £100 for her work, and she eventually donated the tapes to the National Library of Australia. She was further supported by national librarian Sir Harold White, who had been exposed to the concept of oral history on a visit to Columbia University in 1950. White eventually created the National Library of Australia's Oral History Program, initially modeled on Columbia's program and primarily built around the Hazel de Berg collection of interviews. Although there are dimensions of de Berg's project that would not necessarily constitute "best practice" for a contemporary oral history project (she never recorded her questions, for example), this collection of interviews is widely acknowledged as Australia's first formal oral history project.

Some more contemporary oral history projects document a general topic, such as the civil rights movement (for example, Birmingham Civil Rights Institute Oral History Project, Birmingham, Alabama) or veterans of various wars (for example, Imperial War Museum's Oral History Collection, United Kingdom), while other projects document individual experiences, communities, and place, such as the East End Women's Museum Oral History Project documenting the memories, experiences, and lives of women living in London's East End. Other projects focus on documenting specific events, such as the COVID-19 pandemic, the 1964 Civil Rights March in Frankfort, Kentucky, and the terrorist attacks on 9/11 in New York City. Another important style of oral history projects is the life history or biographical approach, where a series of interview sessions focuses on a single individual's life experience and personal memories.

An oral history project consists of much more than a simple aggregation of many interviews. Planning and executing such a project involve numerous decisions about logistics, budget, recording technologies, archiving, and deep consideration of potential legal and ethical issues. Projects have different planning needs, interviewing styles, budgetary needs, and ethical considerations. Although no generic project design template works across various project types, communities, or cultures, there are some basic considerations they should account for. The decisions you make before launching an oral history project may have important implications or consequences that can seriously affect the project outcomes, for better or worse.

The project blueprint

Constructing a "project blueprint" when embarking on the project design phase of an oral history project is helpful. The blueprint will be utilized throughout the project to frame, direct, and assess a project in accordance with the plan. However, like most architectural blueprints, continual evaluation of what works during project implementation and continual revision creates solutions to unforeseen challenges. Again, using the architectural blueprint analogy, drawing the blueprint in advance of project implementation helps visualize the various aspects and phases of the project and envision the outcome.

Appropriate to oral history, one effective method for creating and structuring the oral history project blueprint is in the form of answers to planning questions categorized in the following way: foundational questions, which focus on the purpose of the oral history project; the content and people questions, which explore the story that you intend to document and the central people in that story; the practical questions, which revolve around the logistics and practicalities of implementing an oral history project; the technology and recording questions; the metadata and transcription questions; and finally, the legal and ethical questions, which pertain to the most important considerations when planning an oral history project.

Are you familiar with "best practices"?

Often crafted by practitioners as part of national oral history organizations worldwide, the concept of best practices emerges from the professionalization of oral history. Most of these organizations, on some level, create generalized "best practices" documents to provide guidance and advice for creating oral history projects and conducting interviews. The goals of these "best practices" documents focus on ethical practice, provide technical advice, pose essential considerations for project planning and implementation, provide guidance on oral history interviewing techniques, and explore basic principles involved in the archival goals of access and preservation. Finding the best practices that will suit your oral history project is important.

Within many of these organizations or in regional, national, and international contexts, educational resources exist for learning to "do oral history" within the framework of these best practices, including summer institutes, workshops, and webinars. Because there are different types of oral history projects, prospective project directors should seek out resources that pertain to project goals. For example, the Oral History Association in the United States has published additional documents to supplement their general *Principles and Best Practices* document, including the *Independent Practitioners' Toolkit for Oral Historians*, which contains practical advice and important considerations intended explicitly for "practitioners who work within the field of oral history as freelancers, independent contractors, consultants, artists, community historians, and small business owners." The guide addresses the needs of independent practitioners by guiding various professional and operational aspects of the work. In addition to addressing issues like project funding, the resource provides strategies for marketing services, networking, and building sustainable careers in oral history. The OHA also publishes its *Guidelines for Social Justice Oral History Work*, adopted in 2020, which articulates issues and considerations when designing oral history projects in a social justice framework. Specifically, this set of guidelines presents a framework for ensuring that oral history projects align with principles of equity, representation, and community empowerment, particularly emphasizing creating ethical, inclusive, and collaborative oral history practices that honor the narrators and their communities.

What does "finished" look like?

From the outset of an oral history project, envisioning your ideal and completed project addresses one of the most important foundational questions to consider when designing an oral history project. Before project implementation, it is helpful to acknowledge that the interviews will be used for a specific purpose, such as an academic article or book, a museum exhibit, a podcast episode, or a video documentary.

Sometimes, projects are conducted without specific production outputs in mind, and "finished" means the proper preservation in an archive. In addition to the top-level outputs, it is helpful to envision individual components of a completed project, including consideration of whether the interviews will be transcribed or indexed and the level of descriptive metadata created for each interview, as well as envisioning levels of access to the interviews and whether there are anticipated temporary access restrictions on the interviews. Considering how the narrators and the representative community will perceive the project upon completion is crucial.

Why is this project important?

Writing a project mission statement and answering the question, "Why is this project important?" is very useful during the project design phase. Often derived from a grant application, a project mission statement should include a general project description and specific and realistic project goals. While articulating the project mission statement can be an excellent framing and focusing device, it can also be useful for communicating the importance of your project to others (including potential narrators and funders). Articulating a succinct mission statement with some specificity will assist in developing the core topics and questions asked of the different participants.

The Yiddish Book Center's Wexler Oral History Project concisely states that their project is "expanding collection of in-depth video oral history interviews about Yiddish language and culture. Since 2010, over 1,300 interviews have been recorded with people of all ages and backgrounds around the world. The interviews are used by researchers, artists, and the general public in educational, cultural, and museum settings." This project documents Yiddish language and culture, with a particular focus on creating interviews that a variety of specified audiences in particular settings will use.

The Aqua!Nabara project is a Guanabara Bay oral history project produced by the Urca Institute in Rio de Janeiro, Brazil, that articulates their mission by mentioning the oral history project places "special emphasis on collecting and disseminating plural and oral memories that ultimately make up the broader memory of the territory, aware that the history and knowledge of a territory are personified by these people." Project designers specifically articulate their intended outcomes: "These strategies and contents, the cultural products of this project, are discussed and presented at the seminar *Encontros Água!nabara: Urca Territory*, and disseminated on the website of the *Digital Archive of Affective Memories of Guanabara Bay*."

The following is an example of a mission statement created by project designers for the Black Women in Bourbon (Whiskey) Oral History Project at the University of Kentucky. The project proposed to conduct interviews that are a subset of the larger Women in Bourbon Oral History Project:

> The Black Women in Bourbon Oral History Project furthers the broader goals of the recently launched Women in Bourbon Project, which aims to fill gaps in both scholarly and popular attention to

5. J. Wells interviews Samara Davis, founder of the Black Bourbon Society, for the Black Women in Bourbon Oral History Project, 2022.

> the many women who play key roles in Kentucky's $8.6 billion dollar bourbon industry.... The project includes a variety of women's voices representing multiple perspectives, and was established in partnership with the University of Kentucky's Louie B. Nunn Center for Oral History, and the James B. Beam Institute for Kentucky Spirits.

In addition to providing project focus and clarity, creating a project mission statement and articulating the "why" of a project can also play an important and reflective role in the process of identifying any personal biases or blind spots that project organizers wish to consider going into the project, thus making the project better.

Who will conduct the interviews?

The most significant percentage of oral history projects worldwide are initiated, planned, and implemented by the same individual who then conducts the interviews. Sometimes, however, a project necessitates a team of individuals to plan and conduct the interviews. The most crucial decision in organizing an oral history project is identifying the individual or individuals who will conduct the interviews. Suppose that person is you, fantastic. If that person is unknown, project organizers must identify someone with a broad knowledge of the topic or the community the project represents. The ideal interviewer has the time and the curiosity to conduct comprehensive research, and the project organizers must ensure that the person has the appropriate training to excel at interviewing. It is relatively straightforward to train someone on effective interviewing mechanics. Still, finding someone with the extant knowledge or the commitment to do the extensive and necessary preliminary research is more complicated.

It is essential to consider the interviewer's role and relationship with the individuals or communities they will be engaging with in advance and then make any necessary adjustments to optimize the overall success of the interviews. During the planning process, interviewers should consider their relationship to the oral history project, determine the degree to which they are an insider or outsider, and reflect on the impact of their relationship with the interviewees and the communities represented.

Thinking about what is shared and what is different can be incredibly useful. For example, it can be beneficial for a resident to conduct interviews documenting their local community. The insider knowledge only a local resident will have can effectively generate well-informed questions about esoteric topics that would not be apparent to a community outsider. That said, the person conducting the interview may have a personal relationship with the person interviewed in the local community. When this is the case, the narrator may assume that the interviewer already knows certain esoteric information (and vice versa) and, therefore, does not discuss it. What gets lost is some of the basic contextual community knowledge that would be more openly discussed by an outsider conducting the interview, resulting in an oral history collection that potentially does not contain the necessary information or context for an outsider's complete understanding of the contents of the recorded interview.

A significant disadvantage of the insider interviewer is needing more intentional awareness to ask obvious questions. When training interviewers who are part of the community they will be conducting interviews with, it is essential to emphasize the critical value of recognizing these moments and being comfortable asking the obvious or seemingly "dumb" questions. Rather than be intimidated by one's outsider status, this perspective can be quite advantageous. For example, ask a retired master distiller of bourbon whiskey, "So, explain to me how you make bourbon?" or if one prompts a resident of a community with "Walk me down Main Street on a Saturday night, describe for me the buildings that I would see and the people I would meet?" Although the answers may seem obvious to insiders, playing the outsider card as an interviewer is often very useful and effective.

What is the core content focus?

A common request posed by individuals interested in organizing a local oral history project to those who direct oral history centers is, "Send me your list of questions." Although common question prompts can often be helpful across projects, such as "What do you remember about your "grandparents?" or "How has this community changed throughout your lifetime?," no generic questions will work for every oral history project. Every oral history project is unique, and the memories, experiences, and stories of everyone interviewed for the project will be different.

When designing an oral history project, it is helpful to identify the project's core content to identify the central themes and topics across the interviews. In a biographical life history series of interviews conducted with the same individual, the project core is that person's experiences over a lifetime. Each interview within a project will necessitate a customized subset of questions. However, there will be a continuity of questions that relate to central topics and themes: the project's content core. When an interview begins to digress (and they all digress), it is helpful to remember the project core so that the interview direction can, eventually, be brought back in line with the central themes and topics. Identifying the project core will also help identify and assess the relevant individuals to select for an interview whose stories will best serve the project.

Who will be interviewed?

It seems too obvious, but we must remind ourselves that no oral history project can interview everyone. There must be an assessment and selection process in determining who will be interviewed for any given project. It is useful to ask project planners to think about their oral history project as a story they are writing and consider its principal characters. What are the different roles played by the characters in that story, and what are the different perspectives? For example, if someone were planning an oral history project documenting a locally owned restaurant run by the same family for over fifty years, ask who the most important people would be to interview. The first answer typically focuses on the restaurant's owners. Still, project designers should also consider interviewing the different people who worked at the restaurant over the years—the servers, the greeters, the cooks, and the dishwashers. Another important perspective would be the customers or community members the restaurant serves.

In 2017 project organizers reflected on the planning process for an Oral History of the Electricity Supply Industry in the UK (OHESI), an oral history project run by National Life Stories and archived at the British Library. Acknowledging that there could be an overwhelming number of individuals to select from, project organizers articulate how they refined the selection process:

The aim was to be as representative as possible of this large number of people: documenting different activities, processes and levels, with a good geographical coverage. In practice interviewees were selected through a number of methods. Several had already been identified through the earlier Scoping Study or were noted in the written histories of the industry. Others were identified during ongoing research as being connected to events of significance or selected because the work they did seemed to fill a gap in the project's coverage, aided by the use of a matrix that identified the topics the project needed to cover.

This oral history project utilized an advisory committee to recommend interviewees and serve as "ambassadors" to new potential interviewees. The project also cites the value of the "snowballing" method, where an interviewee suggests other individuals to interview. Beyond interviewee selection, project designers must prioritize the interview list and identify who needs to be interviewed first. Sometimes, it is helpful to prioritize first interviewing individuals in a community who will create additional opportunities to interview others in the community or someone who can provide you with essential background information that will prove useful for additional interviews. It is also important to remember that life is fragile. Thus, it makes sense to prioritize interviewing individuals central to your project, especially those old or sick.

Controversial topics and high-risk content

Controversial topics can emerge in any interview, no matter the topic, including the most seemingly "feel-good" oral history project. It is essential to preemptively consider whether any narrators will discuss "high-risk" topics across the project. For the Oral History of Prostitution, British historian Wendy Rickard in collaboration with the British Library conducted interviews with sex workers in the United Kingdom. Rickard describes the world of sex work as "a fairly secretive subculture where the people move quickly between different roles" and reflects on how participation in interviews in and of itself was "potentially high risk" for the sex workers. Rickard worked with the sex workers and the British Library to establish archival access restrictions as well as a protocol for using aliases for clients referenced in interviews.

For some LGBTQ+ oral history projects, the project directors and interviewers discuss with narrators before the interviews that the project wants to avoid "outing" or publicly identifying other LGBTQ+ individuals who may not wish to be identified. These interview moments are often difficult to anticipate and prepare for in advance. However, when there is a known controversial story in a community, such as a local crime, with rumors about who committed the crime, exploring how interviewers will handle these potentially higher-risk topics should be a fundamental part of project design.

If a recorded interview contains risky or problematic content (posing a risk to the narrators or third-party individuals referenced), the most common way to protect interviews that contain content deemed problematic from an access perspective is by implementing archival access restrictions. The terms of temporary access restriction can vary from the archive requiring special permission for access and use during the narrator's lifetime to simply restricting the interview for a term, such as thirty years. Another approach is using pseudonyms for narrators. However, granular digital access and innovative search technologies significantly complicate the promise of anonymity. Oral history, by nature, contains a massive amount of personal data that can be directly and indirectly associated with individuals even using a pseudonym, especially within the community itself. Sometimes, the high-risk topics are the point of the project; therefore, determining in advance how interviewers should handle these topics and situations is critical.

Recording technologies

Recording technologies have evolved from wax cylinder and wire recorders, reel-to-reel tape recorders, the once-ubiquitous and culturally significant audiocassette, and the fleeting digital audio tape (DAT) and minidisc to file-based digital audio and video recorders. There has been an evolving set of best practices regarding recording oral history interviews, emphasizing the need to create professional-quality recordings optimized for long-term preservation and reuse. Until the COVID-19 pandemic in 2020, the main question from a technology perspective was whether to choose between audio or video recording. Now, the first choice in designing an oral history project is between conducting in-person or remote interviews.

Before the pandemic, "best practices" would have discouraged remote interviews. The argument centered on numerous factors, including the technical quality, as well as the quality of the interview exchange. The remote interaction would be challenging; participants would consistently talk over each other and interrupt, and ultimately, it would not be easy to connect closely with the person you are interviewing and develop rapport in a remote setting such as the telephone or over web conferencing and online interviewing platforms.

However, the pandemic completely changed this perspective. Today, the potential to conduct a remote interview transforms every oral history project into a global oral history project. Web streaming technologies of remote interviewing platforms still do not provide the level of technical quality attainable by in-person recording technologies. However, the convenience and accessibility of remote interviewing platforms have superseded the need to achieve the highest possible recording qualities. Many believe the in-person interview is still the best way to connect with another individual. Still, the remote interview has been

6. Recording equipment that was once commonplace in oral history: the Sony TCM 5000ev Cassette-Corder, the Marantz PMD222 Portable Cassette Recorder, and an audio cassette.

normalized and is a perfectly acceptable method for conducting and recording an oral history interview.

In contemporary oral history practice, audio recordings have been the primary method for recording interviews. There were select examples of video-recorded oral history between the 1940s and early 2000s, but most recorded interviews created in the modern era have been audio recordings. In the analog age, video cameras that met broadcast quality standards were prohibitively expensive. Additionally, academic discussion tended to discount the usefulness of video, questioning the value of recording a "talking head" for long-form oral history interviews. Additionally, there was a great deal of discussion about whether the presence of a video camera potentially changed the dynamic of an interview more significantly than the more subtle audio recorder and microphone setup. Video recording is now affordable and accessible using only a mobile phone. Additionally, the Internet, specifically YouTube and TikTok, has created a revolutionary social and cultural reorientation toward video in most aspects of life, increasing users' and project designers' expectations for video interviews.

Technologically speaking, the "kitchen table" interview, with just an interviewer and a narrator, two microphones, and a professional-quality audio recorder, is one of the simplest methods for recording an oral history interview. To this day, most oral history interviews worldwide still involve audio recordings. However, an increasing percentage of interviews are conducted using professional-quality video. The Yiddish Book Center's Wexler Oral History Project, the Voces Oral History Center at the University of Texas at Austin, and the Cui Yongyuan Center for Oral History, Communications University, in Beijing, China, conduct documentary-quality video oral history interviews for large-scale regional, national, and international projects. For over ten years, the Cui Yongyuan Center conducted over one thousand documentary-quality video interviews averaging over three hours per interview for the Filmmakers of New China Oral History Project, including interviews from a variety of industry perspectives, including actors, executives, technicians, and make-up artists. Centers that have committed to professional-quality video interviewing have mobilized significant resources to do so successfully.

Whether a project chooses audio or video recording for an oral history project, the project designers and interviewers must consider the microphones they will use. Most portable audio recording devices, including mobile phones, have decent built-in microphones. That said, it is still best practice to have professional-quality external microphones and, ideally, to have an individual microphone for each participant in the interview. There are different types of microphones, with differing recording patterns and differences in how microphones connect to your recording device. Microphones can be worn (as is the case with lavalier or lapel microphones) or mounted on stands, and although wired microphones have been the standard, wireless microphones are becoming increasingly popular. Finally, it is best practice to learn, through practice and experimentation, how to optimize the recording through the best microphone placement.

What descriptive metadata will you create for your interviews?

Metadata is, quite simply, data describing data. Creating extensive descriptive metadata for oral history projects and interviews will optimize future researchers' discovery and access experiences. The interview or project that lacks descriptive metadata will remain inaccessible. It is useful to create project workflows that require the interviewers to create initial summaries and descriptive keywords from interviews they conduct. Following the interview, the interviewers and the interviewees are among the few who best know and understand the contents of the interview, so it is best to formalize the interviewers' process of writing summaries, assigning keywords, and creating any relevant notes soon after completing the interview. Creating metadata following an interview will be especially helpful when the interview is accessioned by an archival partner.

Transcribing interviews

Transcribing oral history interviews will profoundly enhance future access and accessibility, yet deciding whether to transcribe an interview has traditionally been challenging. Although the answer should be yes, the cost and labor of creating verbatim transcripts have been prohibitively and increasingly expensive. To compound the problem, the popularity of the oral history methodology has also grown, significantly increasing the volume of interviews being conducted and needing transcription. Although the costs and labor associated with transcription have been intensely limiting for oral history project budgets, this has begun to change.

For years, speech-to-text technologies have been disappointing, creating results that required more time and effort to edit than was worthwhile. It was more cost-effective to pay professional human transcribers. The quantum leap that has taken place since artificial intelligence (AI) capabilities have become mainstream creates an environment where automatically generated draft transcripts have become a reality. Although speech-to-text technologies are rapidly improving, there are still scenarios when professional human transcribers are preferable.

Human transcribers can play an essential role in maintaining confidentiality, mainly when an interview contains archivally "restricted" content or content that the narrator does not want to be made public in the near term in any way. Some interviews and projects require a level of confidentiality in which placing interviews in a cloud computing environment or contributing the content to corporate hosted third-party transcription services could prove risky. Additionally, AI speech-to-text capabilities are only as good as the large language models underlying these systems. Therefore, these systems often do not represent specific languages, dialects, and vernacular speech.

Whether or not human transcribers or machines create transcripts, a first draft will, no doubt, be flawed and require some degree of editing. Since the goal of transcription is the textualization of the recorded interview, the best practice for oral history is the creation of a "verbatim" transcript. While there are multiple oral history style guides and recommendations for representing specific verbal interactions by a particular archive's preferences, there is a strong emphasis on the oral history transcript being a verbatim textualization.

Narrator review

In most cases, it is beneficial to offer the narrators the opportunity to review their interview before it is publicly accessible, whether an oral history interview is transcribed or not. Although the process may significantly slow the project and present prohibitive logistical challenges, this practice fosters greater transparency and a collaborative environment. It provides a greater opportunity for sharing authority and for achieving a better level of informed consent.

The practice of narrator review is especially useful for identifying any content in an interview that a narrator may not recall saying during the interview but, upon review, is uncomfortable with being made public. This added layer provides greater assurance that everyone is comfortable with the content in an archived interview. Additionally, narrator review can be constructive when an interview contains dialects, vernacular speech, and unknown spellings of local entities that prove difficult to transcribe.

Funding and budgetary needs

Oral history projects are sometimes conducted by individuals, sometimes by teams or institutions, sometimes grant-funded, and sometimes without funding. The more common cost categories when planning an oral history project include personnel, equipment, data storage, transcription, indexing, and travel costs.

Although an interview may only last two hours, the interviewer may spend over ten hours researching and preparing for an interview. The interviewer may also need to travel to an interview. In a funded project setting, such as a project sponsored by an oral history center or funded by a grant, ideally, the interviewer's time and efforts are compensated. A typical audio recording kit should contain an audio recorder, two microphones, microphone cables, microphone stands (if not using lavalier microphones), and a cable and adapter to power the recorder.

The decision to record video interviews will typically be more expensive, requiring a camera with professional audio connectivity and lights and light stands used for optimally lighting the interview. If remote interviewing is part of a project, the budget should account for the appropriate service subscriptions. Any oral history planning budget should account for data storage of interviews, especially if there is no archival partner and storage needs will be dramatically larger for video interviews. If there is an archival partner on the project, often they will provide the necessary storage to create data backups while the project is in progress. Finally, an oral history project budget should consider the costs of transcribing and indexing interviews.

Oral history projects range from self-funded projects to large grant-funded projects. Sometimes, oral history projects are privately funded by individuals or foundations, such as Columbia University's Obama Presidency Oral History Project funded by the Obama Foundation. The Nunn Center has utilized private fundraising with stakeholder partners, for example, partnering with the bourbon (whiskey) industry to fund and implement various oral history projects documenting the industry.

There are numerous small and large grant opportunities to fund oral history projects. In the United States, the Kentucky Oral History Commission is a state entity that funds oral history projects, such as the University of Kentucky's Family Farm Oral History Project. In the United Kingdom, the National Lottery Heritage Fund has funded numerous oral history projects over the years, for example, the Hidden Heritage of Wellbeing in the Community: Co-creating Oral Histories of Mental Health Care, an oral history project proposed by Nottingham Trent University in Nottingham, England.

Who are the project partners, and what are their roles?

Many successful oral history projects involve partnerships or collaborations among numerous entities. One can partner with an industry, an organization, or a community. No matter who the partner is, project designers should consider how to best engage the partners and identify the roles of each partner. A common approach to community–partner projects is to create a community advisory board to help guide and inform the oral history project. Advisory boards can help make communities feel like equal partners and create opportunities to interview community members. Engaging the community will most likely complicate projects as there will be disagreement and varying opinions about the project's direction. Still, that is an integral part of the process that will provide community connection and engagement with your project for years.

Do you have an archival partner?

If a project does not have an archival partner, it is strongly recommended that project designers connect with an archive willing to collaborate on your project, preferably in advance of implementation. Once a project is completed, preserving and making interviews available will create endless opportunities for future use and reuse of the interviews in ways the project designers could not imagine. The selected partner archive may have preferences for preferred formats (audio or video), transcription style, or metadata creation standards, but the archive will strongly prefer the types of permissions obtained from narrators. Once more, it is best to engage the archival partner at the beginning of the project and not simply at the end, which ensures project optimization from the future access and preservation perspective. Committing a project to an archive is an important decision; even more important is choosing an archive that comprehensively values oral history and can best preserve and provide future access to your oral history project.

The most important questions: Legal and ethical

One of the most common misconceptions about oral history practice is that it is a feel-good methodology for story collecting. Recording, preserving, and publishing oral history interviews pose potentially significant legal and, more importantly, ethical challenges and considerations. Many of these considerations are situated in national legal frameworks and different cultural contexts.

The guiding principles of the Oral History Association in the United States state that from the interview to the archive, practice must be "guided by respect for narrators and the communities from which they come. This means a commitment to an ethical process and honoring diverse cultural values, ways of knowing, and perspectives." The document stresses the importance of transparency, consent, and collaboration. But to the greatest extent possible, "both the narrator and the interviewer must be protected from harm, particularly those who are vulnerable communities." There is a difference between what is legally allowable and what is ethically responsible. When embarking on an oral history project, one must first deeply consider any potentially relevant legal and ethical issues.

For years, the best resource on the legal implications of oral history practice was the book *A Guide to Oral History and the Law* by oral historian and retired judge John A. Neuenschwander. In this comprehensive book, Neuenschwander explores, from the US perspective, release agreements and copyright, as well as the defamation and privacy risks involved in providing archival access to interviews. This book remains a seminal work on the topic and should be consulted by anyone considering designing an oral history project.

What is "informed consent," and why is it important?

Informed consent ensures that narrators participating in an oral history interview fully understand your motivations for including them in the project and its purpose. Still, narrators must be given a clear frame of reference for how the interview will be made publicly available in the future. It is essential to ensure that each participant fully understands that when an interview goes into the archive, it may someday be made available to a global audience for purposes they may not be able to foresee. It is also essential to convey what it means to "archive" an interview, what rights they are transferring when signing agreements, and their options to limit or impose temporary access restrictions on their interview.

The digital age and the dawning of Internet access to oral history interviews tested the concept of informed consent, as those who signed releases or deeds of gift in the 1970s had no idea of the scale of future distribution of their recording online. Once more, it is important to work with the archival partner early in the process to explore optimal ways for providing informed consent.

Some processes and frameworks, such as specific academic environments, require signed consent forms before the interview.

Informed consent ensures that any participant in an oral history interview understands the future implications of their participation and voluntarily agrees to proceed with the interview. It is helpful to point future interviewees or narrators to online collections so they have a frame of reference and can fully understand how future researchers or online users will engage with their interview.

Interviewers can convey informed consent in a variety of ways. The National Library of Australia provides potential narrators with a full packet explaining the rights agreement, a sample form, a detailed guide for completing the rights agreement form, a sample of their online user agreements, and information about their oral history catalog record. The presentation of the rights agreement form in this packet ensures that narrators fully understand their rights transfer and guides narrators through a detailed series of access levels to their interview to which they can consent or restrict. The National Library of Australia's approach is an excellent example of comprehensively ensuring informed consent. However, other forms of informed consent can be as informal as a detailed conversation prior to the interview.

The "deed of gift," release forms, and copyright

A deed of gift or release form is a legal document that transfers ownership of the recorded interview from the creators of the interview (interviewer and narrator) to the archive or the entity that will be preserving and providing future access to the interview. Once more, consulting the partnering archive about the deed of gift is important for securing the proper and appropriate rights, clarifying future ownership, and clarifying any restrictions to future access. One of the primary functions of the deed of gift or release form is to ensure an archive's ability to provide the interview to future users in ways that can be reproduced in publication, ranging from simple quotations to the reproduction of actual audio excerpts or entire interviews.

There are a variety of deeds of gift and release forms that provide a range of rights and future opportunities. Copyright law in the United States grants the initial interview creators copyright, specifically interpreting the participants in an oral history interview as sharing joint copyright. It is common for deeds of gifts at the institutions to transfer copyright to the recording from the interviewer and narrator to the institution. Copyright transfer will empower the institution to broker future access and empower the institution fully to invest resources toward preserving the interview.

There are other options beyond the transfer of copyright that are less common. Some projects utilize the Creative Commons framework and other licensing agreements where the creators retain ownership but empower the archive through a license agreement to curate the interview fully. That said, many archives with oral history collections do not have the necessary rights, which, unfortunately, places the interview or archival collection into an ambiguous access-limited state. John Neuenschwander states, "The best legal release agreements contain precise but not overly legalistic language, document the full meeting of the minds between the parties on all relevant issues, and provide a roadmap for future use and administration."

What are some of the legal and ethical issues I should consider?

Generally speaking, the legal and ethical goals when conducting oral history interviews should be to do no harm and to minimize risk. Minimizing harm or risk could mean being a sensitive and compassionate interviewer, paying attention to the potential for triggering sensitive or traumatic memories, or fully understanding that the words and phrases used in an oral history interview could negatively impact third parties discussed in an interview. Often, the highest-risk stories in an oral history interview tend to involve third parties, such as when an interviewee accuses another specific individual of a crime or discusses deeply personal details about someone else. These revelations about third parties could be subtle and well-intentioned but could still prove problematic when an interview becomes accessible.

It was one thing to speak about potentially problematic topics in the analog or pre-Internet access age when interviews recorded to audio cassettes often sat in boxes on shelves for decades without anyone requesting access. Today, the contents of an interview can be uploaded, automatically transcribed, and made accessible within just a few hours following the interview. Just as it is essential to provide informed consent, archives must practice "informed accessioning." The archive should be aware of the contents of interviews accessioned into their collections, and they should implement the proper workflows to identify any potentially problematic moments effectively.

By design, some oral history projects pose significant ethical challenges. In the introduction to the book *Listening on the Edge: Oral History in the Aftermath of Crisis*, editor Mark Cave of the Historic New Orleans Collection, writes, "Recording the experience of crisis is central to what the oral historian does, but most commonly such recollections have been captured long after events." However, as evidenced by recent projects documenting September 11, Hurricane Katrina, and the genocide in Rwanda, oral historians have been documenting crisis "soon after, or even in the midst of crisis." Oral history projects must assess and ensure appropriateness, sensitivity, and compassion in addressing trauma in oral history projects. In her article "'First, Do No Harm': Tread Carefully Where Oral History, Trauma, and Current Crisis Intersect," Jennifer A. Cramer, director of the T. Harry Williams

Center at the Louisiana State University, reflects on the context of COVID-19 and the impulse of many oral history practitioners to document the pandemic as it unfolded. Cramer draws upon her experiences during Hurricane Katrina managing crisis-centered oral history projects and poses an important reminder:

> The experience of interviewing someone who recounts an integrated trauma contextualized within decades of a life narrative does not necessarily translate to an interviewer being qualified to conduct crisis-centered oral histories happening in the here and now when people have not had the chance to reflect upon and integrate traumas they are actively experiencing.

Crisis-centered oral history projects often seem enticing at the time of initiation, and project organizers and implementers can be caught up in the project's mission without fully considering the impact on individuals or on their communities.

In specific contexts, primarily academic, more formal mechanisms are necessary for approving a proposed oral history project. Institutional review boards (IRBs) at educational institutions were established in the United States to ensure ethical research practices, particularly in proposed projects involving human subjects. Traditionally, IRBs approve and oversee research studies in medicine and the sciences, focusing on protecting human participants from potential harm. For oral history, however, the relationship with IRBs has been complex. Oral historians often argue that their work differs from scientific research because it prioritizes recording unique personal narratives, shared authority, and co-creation between interviewers and participants rather than testing hypotheses to create generalizable knowledge.

A pivotal development occurred in 2018 with a revision by the US Department of Health and Human Services to the policy, otherwise known as the Common Rule. These changes clarified that oral history and other nongeneralizable work, such as journalism, were to be excluded from IRB oversight. While the updated approach to the review of oral history seemingly alleviates bureaucracy, the core function of IRB was protective, and the complete bypassing of project review by institutions may prove risky. The recommended exclusion of oral history from IRB review does not free oral historians from ethical practice and responsibility. In some ways, the IRB exclusion intensifies the need to broadly communicate professional best practices and ethical frameworks involving oral history projects. For this reason, some institutions in the United States have opted to continue IRB review and required approval for oral history projects.

There is much discussion at oral history conferences and in academic articles about legal and ethical issues pertaining to interviewing; however, there is relatively little discussion about the ethics pertaining to archives and access, especially about narrators' personal information. In 2018 the European Union implemented the General Data Protection Regulation (GDPR), which profoundly impacts oral history projects by imposing legal and ethical requirements for personal data handling in the European Union and the United Kingdom. GDPR emphasizes informed consent, transparency, and safeguarding the rights of interviewees. The tremendous value of GDPR is to protect narrators by formalizing informed consent, articulated through clear agreements detailing data collection and storage from the interview to the archive and the accessibility of the data when an interview becomes publicly available.

GDPR grants individuals rights over their data, including considering access levels to an interview. Ethical safeguards necessitate confidentiality, sensitive data identification and protection, and balancing public access with privacy. While GDPR added multiple layers of bureaucracy to oral history projects in the European Union and the United Kingdom, it is designed to ensure that ethical, legal, and scholarly standards are upheld and protect narrators and their data as best as possible. Whether an oral history project requires IRB approval or is subject to personal data protective frameworks such as GDPR, it is important to more fully consider the potential ethical impacts of a project throughout the planning, interviewing, and archival phases of the oral history lifecycle.

What could possibly go wrong? The Belfast Project

One should consider the Boston College Belfast Project as a case study of what could go wrong. From 2001 to 2006, two Irish journalists conducted oral history interviews documenting the personal experiences of Irish Republican and Loyalist paramilitaries during the time known as "the Troubles" in Northern Ireland. The interviews were archived with Boston College's Burns Library, with the stipulation that interviews would be restricted from public access and the contents kept confidential during the narrators' lifetimes. In short, public knowledge of the existence of the tapes began to proliferate, at which point the Police Service of Northern Ireland (PSNI), through the US Justice Department, subpoenaed Boston College, demanding access to the restricted recordings. After a multiyear judicial process, Boston College released interviews to the British government. Individuals were detained and arrested in subsequent years, and some were convicted. In August 2014 the Oral History Network of Ireland issued an important statement:

> This case emphasises the importance of conducting oral history projects to the highest legal and ethical standards and in particular, the significance of ensuring that all parties (collectors, curators, academic institutions and funding bodies) involved adhere to the principle of informed consent. From the outset of a project, all parties must endeavour to guarantee that the proper procedures and safeguards are in place. It is only by doing so that due care and protection may be provided to all.

Conducting oral history interviews is not a harmless act; it is complex, and it can potentially trigger traumatic memories and document extremely problematic content from both legal and ethical viewpoints. The Belfast Project underscores the need for extensive and thoughtful project planning and preparation.

Upon fully considering the logistical, budgetary, legal, and ethical issues interwoven throughout most oral history projects, ask yourself the final project design question to help craft an effective oral history project: considering all of this, do you still want to implement your oral history project? This chapter began with Hazel de Berg, who, until the end of her life, conducted oral history interviews for what became a monumental national oral history project. When posing the question "What does 'finished' look like?" to help facilitate project planning, this quote from Hazel de Berg's archived personal notes comes to mind. When artist Leonard Hessing was interviewed in September of 1962, de Berg recalled Hessing inquiring about the status of one of her oral history projects, asking, "'Are you finished yet?' to which de Berg recalled saying, 'No,' I said, 'You stop at a point but you are never finished.'"

Chapter 5
The archival impact of oral history

From the project design phase to the moment an interview begins, oral history is about collaborative knowledge creation. The resulting interviews, co-created between interviewers and narrators, contain a massive amount of information that did not exist (in that form) before the interview. However, archiving oral history interviews is not the end of the knowledge-creation process. Although oral history project designers and interviewers often have specific outcomes in mind when implementing a project, the sustainable power of oral history lies in the potential future impacts created by the archive in the acts of preserving and providing future access to these interviews. Archived oral history can shape understanding of the past in ways those who created oral history projects and conducted interviews could not initially imagine.

Donald A. Ritchie's iconic definition of oral history has become a standard reference point for practitioners: "An oral history interview generally consists of a well-prepared interviewer questioning an interviewee and recording their exchange in audio or video format. Interview recordings are transcribed, summarized, indexed, and placed in a library or archives." Ritchie's definition presents three core components: conducting the interview, recording that interview, and placing the interview in a library or archive. Oral history can be a powerful resource for connecting individual stories to the more significant historical record. However, simply conducting an interview will only create the potential for that recorded interview to have an impact. Once an interview is preserved in an archive, the possibilities are endless.

In 2006 Michael Frisch characterized the state of archived oral history interviews as "notoriously underutilized." Frisch was correct; analog interviews in archives worldwide were mostly not digitized, cataloged, or comprehensively described, and most were not transcribed. As a result, researchers rarely accessed interviews. Oral history is a complicated archival resource involving lengthy conversations that are topically unpredictable, involve multiple digressions, and contain natural language and vernacular references—all expressed using accented speech that invariably includes some level of dialect. Given the lack of transcripts or detailed and specific metadata describing the contents of interviews, archives knew relatively little about the rich information contained in the oral history interviews in their collections. Yet the most meaningful value of oral history is often found in those very details.

Archives faced a "discovery" challenge regarding providing access to their oral history interviews, and the usability experience provided by digital library systems at that time was not optimized for time-based resources such as oral history. In 2008, frustrated by the general state of prohibitive access to archived oral histories, the Louie B. Nunn Center for Oral History at the University of Kentucky designed and launched OHMS, the Oral History Metadata Synchronizer, a system to enhance online access to oral history interviews. OHMS synchronized the text in a transcript to the timecode in the audio or video interview, connecting a textual search to the correlating moment in the recorded interview. In addition to enhancing access to transcripts, OHMS offered an indexing module that allowed archives to create searchable chapters or segments in an interview, which contained a range of metadata fields (title, description, keywords, subjects, GPS coordinates) that describe interview details at the "story" level rather than just the interview level. Indexing creates a new level of metadata that dramatically enhances the potential discovery of nuanced details throughout an interview. A narrator could talk about living under segregation for over three hours in an oral history interview without ever saying the actual word "segregation." If a researcher only searched a transcript, they would potentially fail to locate valuable information and then move on to a different resource for their information. An interview index maps natural language to concepts like "segregation" and provides an entirely new dimension to enhance the search and navigation of the interview.

At the time (2008-2009), select archives and institutions were building proprietary systems, often grant-funded, to enhance access to oral histories. These included the indexing and transcript synchronization systems created by the Shoah Foundation, the National Library of Australia, and the University of North Carolina at Chapel Hill. However, these innovative systems were custom-built to only work for their institution, much like the original version of OHMS. In 2012 the University of Kentucky Libraries received a grant to make OHMS a free and open source software solution, and in 2014 they publicly released OHMS for other institutions to use. Fast-forward ten years and OHMS has made a global impact, being utilized by over seven hundred institutions in more than fifty different countries.

As a free platform, OHMS is widely used by institutions of all sizes, from large libraries and archives to smaller cultural heritage organizations. Many institutions, including the Hockey Museum in Surrey, England, the Brooklyn Historical Society, the Yiddish Book Center's Wexler Oral History Project, and archives at the University of Georgia and the University of Wisconsin–Madison take advantage of OHMS. The Palestinian Oral History Archive at the American University of Beirut, the Oral History and Documentation Oral History Project at the American University

7. A 2013 interview with Steve Zahn presented online using the Oral History Metadata Synchronizer.

of Kuwait, and the Academy of Motion Picture Arts and Sciences' Pacific Standard Time: LA/LA Oral History Project all utilize the bilingual capabilities of OHMS to present interviews in multiple languages, thereby increasing the accessibility of oral history.

In the pre-OHMS era, the Nunn Center logged an average of two hundred uses of oral history interviews annually. Since providing access via OHMS, Nunn Center interviews are accessed by a global audience over two hundred thousand times annually. Repositories utilizing systems like OHMS are experiencing a comparable increase in the usage of their archived oral history interviews. Of course, archived oral history continues to be used by scholars in traditional ways, such as conducting research for journal articles and books. However, interviews are now being discovered and used extensively by documentary filmmakers, journalists, and podcasters worldwide. Numerous plays have been written and produced using oral history interviews as the source, and some of the scripts are written verbatim from archived oral history interviews.

Family historians and genealogists are a relatively new audience for accessing and using archived oral history. Enhanced access to oral history has empowered family researchers to discover that interviews with or mentioning family members exist in archives around the world and that there is incredible genealogical information interwoven through most oral history interviews, regardless of the topic of the interview. The Nunn Center's favorite phone calls or email messages involve a family member contacting the staff and thanking the center for its work, making statements such as "I hadn't heard my grandmother's voice for twenty-five years. Hearing her voice brought me such joy."

Classroom engagement with oral history, particularly in higher education settings, has traditionally involved students conducting oral history interviews as part of a course assignment. This experiential model typically assigned students at university or college levels to conduct one-off interviews with family or community members. While this model persists, innovative instances are adding new dimensions to the pedagogical aspects of oral history, extending beyond simply conducting interviews, as the students are engaged in the archival processing phase and actively participate in the process to enhance access to the interviews they conduct. In 2014 professors Charles Hardy and Janneken Smucker from West Chester University taught a course called "Digital Storytelling and the Great Migration to Philadelphia," based on students engaging with archived interviews Hardy conducted between 1982 and 1984. What unfolded over two semesters was a partnership with the archive, training enrolled students on using OHMS to comprehensively index interviews to engage with primary source materials and collaborating with the students to construct an online repository featuring interviews and digital exhibits based on the interviews. The result was an award-winning partnership that created an innovative model for using OHMS as a pedagogical tool for engaging students with oral history as a primary source. Indexing interviews in OHMS requires deep engagement and focused critical thinking. Not only were students doing something they were assigned to do by their professors, but they were actively participating in enhancing access to this oral history project and ensuring that these interviews would more directly impact the historical record and be accessible long into the future.

Another high-level example of oral history as pedagogy is the Mellon Foundation–funded Oral History in the Liberal Arts (OHLA) initiative, created and directed by Brooke Blackmon Bryan. This initiative involves the Great Lakes College Association in the United States and the Global Liberal Arts Alliance, involving nearly thirty small liberal arts schools in the United States and worldwide. Some participating schools include Antioch College, Denison University, and Oberlin University, as well as projects at international institutions, including the Impact of the Family Support System on Female Professionals in Pakistan at Forman Christian College in Pakistan and the Oral History and Cultural Heritage of Morrocco project at Al Akhawayn University in Morrocco. The OHLA model collaborates with faculty and students at partner schools to engage local communities in professional-quality oral history projects, with a particular emphasis on training, best practices, and community engagement. In the OHLA model, the interview is not the endpoint, as oral history projects are transformed into digital projects, enhancing access to interviews using innovative digital tools, including OHMS. OHLA utilizes digital access, often a dedicated website presenting transcribed and indexed oral history interviews, to extend the collaborative aspects of oral history interviewing to a sense of co-creation and reciprocity between the academic institution and the community.

There is no doubt that technological innovation is accelerating. The AI revolution has introduced effective speech-to-text technology to ensure that most interviews can be textualized. Automatically generated transcripts still require significant amounts of cleanup and editing to be made verbatim and accurate; however, the technological tipping point is that it is more cost-effective to generate a transcript and then utilize humans to authenticate it. We are about to see a new revolutionary phase regarding archives' ability to fully process, document, and describe the entirety of oral history collections. Undoubtedly, AI will significantly impact the ability of archives to process and enhance access to archived oral history more effectively and efficiently, creating ever-evolving new usages for archived interviews.

As technological innovation accelerates, we also see the acceleration of potential risks for oral history in the archive. Oral history contains a massive amount of personal information. While privacy issues were already an issue for archived oral histories, the specter of generative AI and its potential impact on oral history practice compounds the issue and should be thoughtfully considered. Archived interviews will be accessed and utilized in ways not initially imagined by project designers, interviewers, or narrators, and some of these usages will not be positive. AI will, undoubtedly, test oral history's concept of "informed consent" in exponentially more complicated ways than the tests posed by merely providing Internet access to online interviews.

The allure of automation is strong. AI technology will be able to help oral historians by creating draft transcripts, comprehensive descriptive metadata, and draft OHMS indexes for every interview. However, not every interview should be made publicly available. AI technology can also evaluate an interview to identify sensitive or potentially problematic content that could pose risks to narrators, third-party individuals referenced in interviews, and communities. Given the deeply personal nature of what is discussed in even the most seemingly harmless oral history interview, we must thoughtfully and actively consider new best practices that focus on creating frameworks for providing ethical access to these important oral history collections.

In February 2013 a researcher named Giovanni Caruso living in Tremensuoli, a small village in Italy situated on the coast about ninety kilometers north of Naples, contacted the Nunn Center. Caruso declared he was considering writing a book based on local experiences of American soldiers in Tremensuoli during World War II, and he requested the Nunn Center's 1986 interview with Marshall A. Webb from the American Veterans: World War II Oral History Project.

Marshall Webb was from Campbellsville, Kentucky, and had varying experiences during World War II, including service in North Africa and Italy, as well as being in one of the first groups to enter the Dachau concentration camp following liberation. As the Allies moved north to take Rome, there were significant battles in Tremensuoli and the surrounding areas of that region of Italy. Marshall Webb participated in those battles. The archival description of Webb's interview mentions that he "reads a poem he wrote about the Battle of Tremensuoli." In fact, in the fifty-second minute of the interview, Webb recites a poem that he wrote about his personal experiences during the battle. It is safe to say that most World War II veterans did not break out into poetry readings during oral history interviews, so this was rather unusual. Nevertheless, we were able to provide the researcher access to this interview.

I assumed at the time that Caruso had Googled "Tremensuoli" and "World War II" or something similar, and thanks to an archival framework optimized for discovery, he was successful. Proud that the discovery system worked, Nunn Center staff asked the researcher whether he wanted them to search for any other interviews in the collection that might relate to his topic, an offer the researcher promptly and politely declined. This answer seemed unusual, as most researchers working on a writing project typically want the archive to find anything and everything even remotely relevant to their research topic. However, this researcher did not want any oral history interview conducted with a veteran who served in Tremensuoli; he specifically wanted the interview with Marshall Webb. Sensing that there was more to this story, we curiously inquired why he was interested in just Marshall Webb's interview. When the researcher responded, he attached a photograph to the email message. The first photograph was of a small alley in Tremensuoli lined with stone row houses on a slight hill. The second photograph showed a close-up picture of the wall of one of the row houses, on which was clearly carved: "MA Webb, C-Ville KY. 1944 March 30." Marshal Webb from Campbellsville, Kentucky, off fighting in a small village in Italy, half a world from Campbellsville, Kentucky, on March 30, 1944, carved his name on the wall in that alley. After he was able to identify "C-Ville KY" as Campbellsville, Kentucky, Caruso triangulated Marshall Webb's nearly seventy-year-old graffiti to the Nunn Center's four-hour interview in the archive.

Marshall Webb passed away in 2004. However, the Nunn Center connected with Webb's family and conducted interviews in Campbellsville with Opal Webb, Marshall's widow, and their son, Roger Webb, who had driven down from Chicago. Mrs. Webb talked about Marshall, their family, and their lives together. She talked about Marshall's poetry and how he did not think of himself as a poet, but he wrote over eighty poems throughout the war. After that meeting, the Webb family donated Marshall Webb's poetry and World War II photographs to the Special Collections Research Center, University of Kentucky Libraries,

8. The wall where Marshall A. Webb carved his name on March 30, 1944, in Tremensuoli, Italy.

which now has comprehensive documentation of Marshall Webb's personal experiences during World War II.

When reflecting on this experience, one could chalk it up to being one of those "it's a small world after all" experiences, but it is so much more than that. In 1986 Colonel Arthur L. Kelly asked Marshall Webb if he would participate in an oral history interview for Kelly's oral history project documenting the experiences of Kentucky's World War II veterans. Webb consented and participated in a powerful and detailed, nearly four-hour-long interview. Most of that interview very much centered on Webb's experiences following the liberation of Dachau; in fact, Webb's experience in Tremensuoli was a relatively brief topic in the interview. It was such a minor topic that it might not have been represented in the interview description if Webb had not recited the poem mid-interview. Since the release of this story, Caruso and Tremensuoli officials protected the carving behind mounted plexiglass and hung an informational sign next to Webb's carving. The sign has a photograph of Marshall Webb, including the text of his poem "The Battle of Tremensuoli." Below the poem is a link to the OHMS-ed interview online, where a visitor can stand in that alley with a mobile phone and listen to the moment Marshall Webb reads that poem. In January 2025 I was finally able to travel to Tremensuoli, Italy, meet with Giovanni Caruso for the first time, stand quietly before Marshall Webb's carving, and then spend many hours walking the streets with Caruso and sharing stories.

Yes, one must first conduct the oral history interview they are considering conducting with a mother or father or a community member before it is too late. However, simply conducting the interview only creates the potential to add an individual story to the historical record. There is so much more to the oral history process than merely buying a recorder and asking someone questions. Explore oral history's best practices, thoroughly research the interview you plan to conduct, go through the project design process and create that project blueprint, establish an archival partnership to ensure that future discoveries like the Marshall Webb discovery will be possible, and then sit down with your first narrator or interviewee, press the record button on your recorder, and ask that first question, "Tell me a little about yourself."

References

Chapter 1: Tell me a little about yourself

William B. Hesseltine, Vaughan Bornet, Owen Bombard, Frank Ernest Hill, and Fred A. Shannon, "Is Oral History Really Worth While?" in *Ideas in Conflict: A Colloquium on Certain Problems in Historical Society Work* (Harrisburg, PA: American Association for State and Local History, 1958): 17, 4, 34–35.

Paul Thompson, *The Voice of the Past: Oral History* (Oxford: Oxford University Press, 1978), 18.

Zora Neale Hurston, *Barracoon: The Story of the Last "Black Cargo,"* ed. Deborah G. Plant (New York: Amistad, an imprint of HarperCollins, 2018), xiv.

Sharon Tanagi Aburano, interview by Tom Ikeda, April 3, 2008, *Densho Visual History Collection*, Densho.

Wonga Tabata, "The South African History Project (SAHP) of the Department of Education—A Reflection on Achievements, Challenges and Opportunities: 2001-2006," *Oral History Journal of South Africa* 3, no. 1 (2015): 15–24.

Jinja Moore, "Voices of Rwanda: Healing the Wounds of Genocide," *Christian Science Monitor* (December 4, 2008).

Taylor Krauss, "In the Ghost Forest: Listening to Tutsi Rescapés," in *Listening on the Edge: Oral History in the Aftermath of Crisis*, ed. Mark Cave and Stephen M. Sloan (New York: Oxford Oral History Series, Oxford University Press), 107.

Martin Luther King Jr., interview by Robert Penn Warren, March 18, 1964, *"Who Speaks for the Negro?" The Robert Penn Warren Civil Rights Oral History Project*, Louie B. Nunn Center for Oral History, University of Kentucky Libraries.

Chapter 2: Defining oral history through time

James Boswell, *The Journal of a Tour to the Hebrides with Samuel Johnson, LL.D* (London: J. M. Dent & Co.; E. P. Dutton & Co., 1909), 384.

Paul Thompson with Joanna Bornat, *The Voice of the Past: Oral History. The Voice of the Past: Oral History*, 4th ed. (New York: Oxford University Press, 2017), 23.

Linda Shopes, "Making Sense of Oral History," in *History Matters*, https://historymatters.gmu.edu/mse/oral/ (accessed December 1, 2024).

Charles T. Morrissey, "Riding a Mule Through the 'Terminological Jungle': Oral History and Problems of Nomenclature," *Oral History Review* 12, no. 1 (1984): 13–28.

Allan Nevins, *The Gateway to History* (Boston: D.C. Heath, 1938), iv.

Elizabeth I. Dixon and James V. Mink, *Oral History at Arrowhead: The Proceedings of the First National Colloquium on Oral History* (Los Angeles: Oral History Association, 1969), 4.

Willa K. Baum, *Oral History for the Local Historical Society* (American Association for State and Local History by special arrangement with the Conference of California Historical Societies, 1974), 1.

Ronald J. Grele, "Directions for Oral History in the United States," in *Oral History: An Interdisciplinary Anthology*, ed. David K. Dunaway and Willa K. Baum (Walnut Creek, CA: Altamira Press, 1996), 62–84.

D. Chew (ed.), *Memories and Reflections: The Singapore Experience— Documenting a Nation's History Through Oral History* (Singapore: Oral History Centre, National Archives of Singapore, 2007), 1.

Donald A. Ritchie, *Doing Oral History*, 3rd ed. (New York: Oxford University Press, 2014), 1.

Daniel Defoe, *A Tour Thro' the Whole Island of Great Britain: Divided into Circuits or Journies*, Volume II, Letter I (London, 1725), 6.

"An Account of Island Magee, Taken in 1809," *The Belfast Monthly Magazine* 3, no. 13 (1809): 104–6.

"Indians on the Northwest Frontier," *Adams Sentinel* (Gettysburg, PA, July 17, 1827), 4.

"A Guide to the Giants' Causeway," *Dublin Penny Journal* 2 (1834), ix–xvi.

Robert H. Lowie, "Oral Tradition and History," *Journal of American Folklore* 30, no. 116 (1917): 161–67.

Richard M. Dorson, "The Oral Historian and the Folklorist," in *Selections from the Fifth and Sixth National Colloquia on Oral History, Indiana University, Bloomington, IN, October 8–10, 1971*, ed. Peter D. Olch and Forrest C. Pogue (Los Angeles: Oral History Association, 1972), 40.

Hugh Trevor-Roper's statement was originally made in 1963 during a lecture at the University of Sussex and transmitted by BBC Television. The lectures appeared in print in *The Listener* in 1963 and were eventually published in 1965 in his book *The Rise of Christian Europe*, published by Thames and Hudson (London).

Marshall Sahlins, "Other Times, Other Customs: The Anthropology," *American Anthropologist* 85 (1983): 198.

S. O. Biobaku, "The Problem of Traditional History with Special Reference to Yoruba Traditions," *Journal of the Historical Society of Nigeria* 1, no. 1 (1956): 43–47.

Thucydides, *The History of the Peloponnesian War*, trans. Richard Crawley (London: J. M. Dent and Co., 1914), 15.

A. M. Sellar, *Bede's Ecclesiastical History of England: A Revised Translation with Introduction, Life, and Notes* (London: George Bell and Sons, 1907), 4.

Bernardino de Sahagún, *Historia general de las Cosas de Nueva España*, 1577. *General History of the Things of New Spain by Fray Bernardino de Sahagún: The Florentine Codex. Book XII: The Conquest of Mexico*, trans. Arthur J. O. Anderson and Charles E. Dibble (Salt Lake City: University of Utah Press, 1955).

Jules Michelet, *Historical View of the French Revolution, From its Earliest Indications to the Flight of the King in 1791*, trans. C. Cocks B.L. (London: G. Bell, 1902), 10.

Letter to the editor, John Fanning Watson titled "Old Times," *Poulson's American Daily Advertiser*, March 6, 1821. This issue of the newspaper was obtained from the Wisconsin Historical Society.

John Fanning Watson, "Trip to Reading—1825," personal journal, *Watson Family Diaries Collection*, Winterthur Library.

Deborah Norris Logan, Diary No. 11, March 17, 1827, Historical Society of Pennsylvania, 32.

William B. Hesseltine, *Pioneer's Mission: The Story of Lyman Copeland Draper* (Madison: State Historical Society of Wisconsin, 1954), 153.

Ruben Gold Thwaites, *How George Rogers Clark won the Northwest and Other Essays in Western History* (Chicago: A.C. McClurg, 1903), 342.

William W. Moss, "Oral History: What Is It and Where Did It Come From?" In *The Past Meets the Present: Essays on Oral History*, ed. David Stricklin and Rebecca Sharpless (Lanham, MD: University Press of America, 1988), 6.

Thomas A. Edison, "The Phonograph and Its Future," *The North American Review* 126, no. 262 (1878): 527–36.

"National Academy of Sciences. An Interesting Session Yesterday—Edison, the Modern Magician Unfolds the Mysteries of the Phonograph," *Evening Star*, April 19, 1878.

Ann Banks, "Introduction," in *First-Person America* (New York: Norton, 1991), xi–xxv.

Lynda M. Hill, "Ex-Slave Narratives: The WPA Federal Writers' Project Reappraised," *Oral History* 26, no. 1 (1998): 64–72.

Charles T. Morrissey, "Why Call It 'Oral History': Searching for an Early Usage of a Generic Term," *Oral History Review* 8, no. 1 (1980): 20–48.

Charles Francis Hall, *Charles Francis Hall Journal with Navigational Notes 1861*, Smithsonian Institution Archives Center (NMAH, 1861).

Horace Gregory, "Pepys on the Bowery," *New Republic*, April 15, 1931, 249.

Joseph Mitchell, "Professor Sea Gull," *New Yorker*, December 12, 1942.

Jill Lepore, *Joe Gould's Teeth* (New York: Knopf, 2016), 132.

Allan Nevins, interview by Frank Ernest Hill, in *Individual Interviews: Oral History Collection* (New York: Columbia Center for Oral History, Columbia University, 1963), 236.

Gary L. Shumway, *Oral History in the United States: A Directory* (Los Angeles: Oral History Association, 1971).

Allan Nevins, *Gateway to History* (Boston: Heath and Company, 1938), iv.

Sherna Gluck, "What's So Special About Women? Women's Oral History," *Frontiers: A Journal of Women Studies* 2, no. 2 (1977): 3–17.

Sherna Gluck, "Reflections on Oral History in the New Millennium: Roundtable Comments from First Generation Oral Historians to Fourth and Beyond," *Oral History Review* 26, no. 2 (1999): 3.

Oral History Society, "The History of Oral History," https://www.ohs.org.uk/about-2/ (accessed December 1, 2024).

Rebecca Sharpless, "The History of Oral History," in *Handbook of Oral History*, ed. Thomas L. Charlton, Lois E. Meyers, and Rebecca Sharpless (Lanham, MD: Altamira Press, 2006), 20.

Barbara Wertheim Tuchman, "Distinguishing the Significant from the Insignificant," *Radcliffe Quarterly* 56, no. 1 (March 1977): 10.

Eric Hobsbawm, *On History* (London: Weidenfeld and Nicolson, 1997), 206.

Alessandro Portelli, "The Death of Luigi Trastulli and Other Stories: Form and Meaning in Oral History," (Albany: State University of New York Press, 1991), 26.

Oral History Association, "Oral History: Defined," https://oralhistory.org/about/do-oral-history/ (accessed December 1, 2024).

Nepia Mahuika, *Rethinking Oral History and Tradition: An Indigenous Perspective* (New York: Oxford University Press, 2019), 1.

Kristina R. Llewellyn, Alexander Freund, and Nolan Reilly, *The Canadian Oral History Reader* (Montreal: McGill-Queen's Press, 2015), 4.

Alistair Thomson, "Fifty Years On: An International Perspective on Oral History," *Journal of American History* 85, no. 2 (1988): 581–95.

Chapter 3: Asking questions: The oral history interview

Paul Thompson with Joanna Bornat, *The Voice of the Past: Oral History*, 4th ed. (New York: Oxford University Press, 2017), 308.

Alessandro Portelli, "Thirty Years of Field Work in Harlan County: Oral History and Dialogue." Lecture presented at the University of Kentucky Libraries 27th Edward F. Prichard Lecture, University of Kentucky, October 26, 2010.

Alessandro Portelli, *The Battle of Valle Giulia: Oral History and the Art of Dialogue* (Madison: University of Wisconsin Press, 1997), 4.

Alessandro Portelli, *The Death of Luigi Trastulli and Other Stories: Form and Meaning in Oral History* (Albany: State University of New York Press, 1991), 46–58.

Lynn Abrams, *Oral History Theory* (London: Routledge, 2010), 58.

Sherna Gluck, "What's So Special About Women? Women's Oral History," *Frontiers: A Journal of Women Studies* 2, no. 2 (1977): 3–17.

Kathryn Anderson and Dana Jack, "Learning to Listen: Interview Techniques and Analyses," in *Women's Words: The Feminist Practice of Oral History*, 1st ed. (New York: Routledge, 1991), 17–32.

Mark Feldstein, "Kissing Cousins: Journalism and Oral History," *The Oral History Review* 31, no. 1 (2004): 1–22.

"Principles and Best Practices," *Oral History Association* (2009), https://oralhistory.org/about/principles-and-practices-revised-2009/ (accessed December 1, 2024).

As a young oral historian about to teach an interviewing workshop, I found this "leading the witness" example in an oral history interview in the "County Collections" part of the oral history collection at the Kentucky Historical Society. In haste, I excerpted the audio (which I continue to use in workshops to this day) and neglected to note the original interview citation. I have used this audio excerpt in workshops for nearly twenty years. I have tried to reidentify the unidentified person in this recording, but I have yet to find the original citation.

Ralph J. Devine, interview by Arthur L. Kelly, March 11, 1994, *American Veterans: World War Two Oral History Project*, Louie B. Nunn Center for Oral History, University of Kentucky Libraries.

Beulah Collins, interview by Charles Hardy III., August 1, 1983, *Goin' North: Tales of the Great Migration Oral History Project*, Louie B. Nunn Center for Oral History, University of Kentucky Libraries.

Charles T. Morrissey, "The Two-Sentence Format as an Interviewing Technique in Oral History Fieldwork," *Oral History Review* 15, no. 1 (1987): 43–53.

Shirley Manson, interviewed by Tanya Pearson, February 8, 2018, Smith College Libraries.

Steve Zahn, interview by Douglas A. Boyd, May 29, 2013, *American Veterans: From Combat to Kentucky, Student Veteran Oral History Project*, Louie B. Nunn Center for Oral History, University of Kentucky Libraries.

Chapter 4: Designing an oral history project

Diana Ritch, "My Mother, Hazel de Berg, Oral History Pioneer," *The Oral History Association of Australia Journal* 18 (1996): 29–36.

"Independent Practitioners' Toolkit for Oral Historians," *Oral History Association* (2021). https://oralhistory.org/best-practices-guidelines-and-toolkits/ (accessed December 1, 2024).

"Guidelines for Social Justice Oral History Work," *Oral History Association* (2020). https://oralhistory.org/guidelines-for-social-justice-oral-history-work/ (accessed December 1, 2024).

The specific phrase "What does 'Finished' look like" in this context emerges from a workshop created and led by oral historians Jennifer Cramer, Troy Reeves, and Doug Boyd.

The project mission for the Yiddish Book Center's Wexler Oral History Project was emailed to the author by request from Christa Whitney, the project director of the Wexler Oral History Project.

"The Água!nabara Collection," Urca Institute. https://aguanabara.org/o-projeto/ (accessed December 1, 2024).

The mission statement for the Black Women in Bourbon (Whiskey) Oral History Project is quoted from the IRB application submitted by project creators Janice Fernheimer, J. Wells, and Doug Boyd.

National Life Stories in partnership with the British Library, "An Oral History of the Electricity Supply Industry in the UK: Final Report" (2017), 4.

Wendy Rickard, "Collaborating with Sex Workers in Oral History," *Oral History Review* 3, no. 1 (2003): 47–59.

"OHA Core Principals," Oral History Association, https://oralhistory.org/oha-core-principles/ (accessed December 1, 2024).

Doug Boyd, "Informed Accessioning: Questions to Ask After the Interview," in *Oral History in the Digital Age*, ed. Doug Boyd, Steve Cohen, Brad Rakerd, and Dean Rehberger (Washington, DC: Institute of Museum and Library Services, May 2015). https://ohda.matrix.msu.edu/2015/03/informed-accessioning-questions-to-ask-after-the-interview/ (accessed December 1, 2024)

John A. Neuenschwander, "The Legal Ramifications of Oral History," in *The Oxford Handbook of Oral History*, ed. Donald A. Ritchie (New York: Oxford University Press, 2011), 353.

Mark Cave, "What Remains: Reflections on Crisis Oral History," in *Listening on the Edge: Oral History in the Aftermath of Crisis*, ed. Mark Cave and Stephen M. Sloan (New York: Oxford University Press, 2014), 1.

Jennifer A Cramer, "'First, Do No Harm': Tread Carefully Where Oral History, Trauma, and Current Crises Intersect," *Oral History Review* 47, no. 2 (July 2, 2020): 203–13.

"Statement by the Oral History Network of Ireland on the Boston College Belfast Project," *Oral History Network of Ireland (OHNI)*, August 2014, https://oralhistorynetworkireland.ie/wp-content/uploads/2020/09/OHNI-Statement-on-Boston-College-Aug-2014.pdf (Accessed December 1, 2024).

Hazel de Berg, *Hazel de Berg Interviewing Notes (1960–1963, Oral History and Folklore Collection*, National Library of Australia. The note accompanies the record pertaining to the interview with Leonard Hessing in September 1962.

Chapter 5: The archival impact of oral history

Donald A. Ritchie, *Doing Oral History*, 3rd ed. (New York: Oxford University Press, 2014), 1.

Michael Frisch, "Oral History and the Digital Revolution: Toward a Post-Documentary Sensibility," in *Oral History Reader*, 2nd ed., ed. Robert Perks and Alistair Thomson (London: Routledge, 2006), 102.

Douglas A. Boyd, Janice W. Fernheimer, and Rachel Dixon. "Indexing as Engaging Oral History Research: Using OHMS to 'Compose History' in the Writing Classroom." *Oral History Review* 42, no. 2 (2015): 352-367. This article describes the first archive-classroom partnership using OHMS as a pedagogical tool involving the Nunn Center, Doug Boyd, and Janice Fernheimer.

Janneken Smucker, Doug Boyd, and Charles Hardy III, "Connecting the Classroom and the Archive: Oral History, Pedagogy, & Goin' North," in *Oral History in the Digital Age*, ed. Doug Boyd, Steve Cohen, Brad Rakerd, and Dean Rehberger (Washington, DC: Institute of Museum and Library Services, 2017), https://ohda.matrix.msu.edu/2017/02/connecting-the-classroom-and-the-archive-oral-history-pedagogy-goin-north/ (accessed December 1, 2024).

Todd Moye., "Goin' North: Stories from the Great Migration to Philadelphia," media review, *Oral History Review* 43, no. 2 (September 1, 2016): 425–27.

Marshall Webb interview by Arthur L. Kelly, January 16, 1986, *American Veterans: World War Two Oral History Project*, Louie B. Nunn Center for Oral History, University of Kentucky Libraries.

Further reading

About Oral History

Abrams, Lynn. *Oral History Theory*. 2nd ed. London: Routledge, 2016.

Boyd, Douglas A., and Mary Larson, eds. *Oral History and Digital Humanities: Voice, Access, and Engagement*. 1st ed. New York: Palgrave Macmillan, 2014.

Boyd, Nan Alamilla, and Horacio N. Roque Ramirez. *Bodies of Evidence: The Practice of Queer Oral History*. New York: Oxford University Press, 2012.

Carey Jr., David. *Oral History in Latin America: Unlocking the Spoken Archive*. Philadelphia: Taylor & Francis, 2017.

Cave, Mark, and Stephen M. Sloan. *Listening on the Edge: Oral History in the Aftermath of Crisis*. New York: Oxford University Press, 2014.

Charlton, Thomas Lee, Lois E. Myers, and Rebecca Sharpless. *Thinking About Oral History: Theories and Applications*. Walnut Creek, CA: Altamira Press, 2008.

Dunaway, David K., and Willa K. Baum, eds. *Oral History: An Interdisciplinary Anthology*. American Association for State and Local History Book Series. Walnut Creek, CA: Altamira Press, 1996.

Frisch, Michael. *A Shared Authority: Essays on the Craft and Meaning of Oral and Public History*. Albany: State University of New York Press, 1990.

Gluck, Sherna Berger, and Daphne Patai. *Women's Words: The Feminist Practice of Oral History*. London: Routledge, 1991.

Grele, Ronald J., *Envelopes of Sound: The Art of Oral History*. London: Bloomsbury Academic, 1991.

Hamilton, Paula, and Linda Shopes. *Oral History and Public Memories*. Philadelphia: Temple University Press, 2009.

High, Steven, *Beyond Testimony and Trauma: Oral History in the Aftermath of Mass Violence*. Vancouver: UBC Press, 2015.

Llewellyn, Kristina R., Alexander Freund, and Nolan Reilly. *The Canadian Oral History Reader*. Montreal: McGill-Queen's Press, 2015.

Mahuika, Nepia. *Rethinking Oral History and Tradition: An Indigenous Perspective*. New York: Oxford University Press, 2019.

Perks, Robert, and Alistair Thomson. *The Oral History Reader*. 3rd ed. New York: Routledge, 2016.

Portelli, Alessandro, The *Death of Luigi Trastulli and Other Stories: Form and Meaning in Oral History*. Albany: State University of New York Press, 1991.

Portelli, Alessandro. *The Battle of Valle Giulia: Oral History and the Art of Dialogue*. Madison: University of Wisconsin Press, 1997.

Ritchie, Donald A. *The Oxford Handbook of Oral History*. New York: Oxford University Press, 2012.

Ritchie, Donald A. *Doing Oral History*. 3rd ed. New York: Oxford University Press, 2014.

Sheftel, A., and Stacey Zembrzycki. *Oral History Off the Record: Toward an Ethnography of Practice*. New York: Springer, 2013.

Srigley, Katrina, Stacey Zembrzycki, and Franca Iacovetta. *Beyond Women's Words: Feminisms and the Practices of Oral History in the Twenty-First Century*. London: Routledge, 2018.

Summerskill, Clare, Amy Tooth Murphy, and Emma Vickers. *New Directions in Queer Oral History: Archives of Disruption*. London: Routledge, 2022.

Thompson, Paul with Joanna Bornat. *The Voice of the Past: Oral History*. 4th ed. New York: Oxford University Press, 2017.

Vansina, Jan M. *Oral Tradition as History*. Madison: University of Wisconsin Press, 1985.

Oral History Practice

Barnett, Teresa, and Chon A. Noriega. *Oral History and Communities of Color*. Los Angeles: UCLA Chicano Studies Research Center Press, 2013.

Barnickel, Linda. *Oral History for the Family Historian: A Basic Guide*. Los Angeles: Oral History Association, 2006.

Baum, Willa K. *Transcribing and Editing Oral History*. Walnut Creek, CA: Altamira Press, 1977.

Chew, D. (ed.). *Memories and Reflections: The Singapore Experience—Documenting a Nation's History Through Oral History*. Singapore: Oral History Centre, National Archives of Singapore, 2007.

Freund, Alexander, and Alistair Thomson, eds. *Oral History and Photography*. New York: Palgrave Studies in Oral History, 2011.

Hutching, M. *Talking History: A Short Guide to Oral History*. Wellington, New Zealand: Bridget Williams Books/Historical Branch of the Department of Internal Affairs, 1993.

Ives, Edward D. *The Tape-Recorded Interview: A Manual for Fieldworkers in Folklore and Oral History*. 2nd ed. Knoxville: University of Tennessee Press, 1995.

Mackay, Nancy. *Curating Oral Histories: From Interview to Archive*. Walnut Creek, CA: Left Coast Press, 2007.

Mackay, Nancy, Mary Kay Quinlan, and Barbara Sommer. *Community Oral History Toolkit*. Walnut Creek, CA: Left Coast Press, 2013.

Neuenschwander, John A. *A Guide to Oral History and the Law*. New York: Oxford University Press, 2014.

Robertson, Beth M. *Oral History Handbook*. Oral History Association of Australia (South Australian Branch), 2006.

Sommer, Barbara W., and Mary Kay Quinlan. *The Oral History Manual*. Walnut Creek, CA: Altamira Press, 2002.

Yow, Valerie Raleigh. *Recording Oral History: A Practical Guide for Social Scientists*. Thousand Oaks, CA: Sage, 1994.

Using Oral History Interviews

Boyd, Douglas A. *Crawfish Bottom: Recovering a Lost Kentucky Community*. Lexington: University Press of Kentucky, 2011.

Clark, Mary Marshall, Peter Bearman, Catherine Ellis, and Stephen Drury Smith. *After the Fall: New Yorkers Remember September 2001 and the Years That Followed*. New York: New Press, 2016.

Cruikshank, J. *The Social Life of Stories: Narrative and Knowledge in the Yukon Territory*. Lincoln: University of Nebraska Press, 1998.

Dawson, Grahama, Kim Lacy Rogers, and Selma Leydesdorff. *Trauma and Life Stories*. London: Routledge, 2000.

Denis, P., and R. Ntsimane (eds.). *Oral History in a Wounded Country: Interactive Interviewing in South Africa*. Durban: University of KwaZulu-Natal Press, 2008.

Field, Sean. *Lost Communities, Living Memories: Remembering Forced Removals in Cape Town*. Cape Town: David Philip, 2001.

Field, Sean. *Oral History, Community and Displacement: Imagining Memories in Post-Apartheid South Africa*. New York: Palgrave Macmillan, 2012.

Fosl, Catherine, and Tracy E. K'Meyer. *Freedom on the Border: An Oral History of the Civil Rights Movement in Kentucky*. Lexington: University Press of Kentucky, 2009.

Gluck, Sherna Berger. *Rosie the Riveter Revisited: Women, the War, and Social Change*. Boston: Twayne, 1987.

Greenwhich, Alex, and Shirlene Robinson. *Yes Yes Yes: Australia's Journey to Marriage Equality*. Sydney: University of New South Wales Press, 2018.

High, Steven. *Oral History at the Crossroads: Sharing Life Stories of Survival and Displacement* (Vancouver: UBC Press, 2014).

High, S., E. Little, and T. R. Duong (eds.). *Remembering Mass Violence: Oral History, New Media and Performance*. Toronto: University of Toronto Press, 2014.

Huen, P. L. P., J. H. Morrison, and K. C. Guan (eds.). *Oral History in Southeast Asia: Theory and Method*. Singapore: National Archives of Singapore and Institute of Southeast Asian Studies, 1998.

Ilic, M., and D. Leinarte, D. (eds.). *The Soviet Past in the Post-Socialist Present: Methodology and Ethics in Russian, Baltic and Central European Oral History and Memory Studies*. London: Routledge, 2016.

Johnson, E. Patrick. *Black. Queer. Southern. Women.: An Oral History*. Chapel Hill: University of North Carolina Press, 2018.

Khanenko-Friesen, Natalia, and Gelinada Grinchenko. *Reclaiming the Personal: Oral History in Post-Socialist Europe*. Toronto: University of Toronto Press, 2015.

Lanzmann, C. *Shoah: An Oral History of the Holocaust*. New York: Pantheon, 1985.

Lee, Debbie, and Kathryn Newfont (eds.). *The Land Speaks: New Voices at the Intersection of Oral and Environmental History*. Oxford Oral History Series. New York: Oxford University Press, 2017.

Loh, K. S., E. Koh, and S. Dobbs (eds.). *Oral History in Southeast Asian: Memories and Fragments*. New York: Palgrave Macmillan, 2013.

Meihy, J. C. S. B. (ed.) *(Re)introduzindo a História Oral no Brasil*. São Paulo: Xamã, 1996.

Miller, B. G. *Oral History on Trial: Recognizing Aboriginal Narratives in the Courts*. Vancouver: UBC Press, 2011.

Montell, William Lynwood. *The Saga of Coe Ridge; a Study in Oral History*. 1st ed. Knoxville: University of Tennessee Press, 1970.

Moye, J. Todd. *Freedom Flyers: The Tuskegee Airmen of World War II*. New York: Oxford University Press, 2012.

Ortiz, Paul. *An African American and Latinx History of the United States*. Boston: Beacon Press, 2018.

Passerini, Luisa. *Fascism in Popular Memory: The Cultural Experience of the Turin Working Class*. Cambridge: Cambridge University Press, 1987.

Passerini, Luisa (ed.). *International Yearbook of Oral History and Life Stories. Vol. I: Memory and Totalitarianism*. Oxford: Oxford University Press, 1992.

Pollock, D. *Remembering: Oral History Performance*. New York: Springer, 2017.

Portelli, Alessandro. *The Order Has Been Carried Out: History, Memory, and Meaning of a Nazi Massacre in Rome*. New York: Palgrave Macmillan, 2003.

Puri, Anisa, and Alistair Thomson. *Australian Lives: An Intimate History*. Clayton, Australia: Monash University Publishing, 2017.

Rosen, A. *The Wonder of Their Voices: The 1946 Holocaust Interviews of David Boder*. New York: Oxford University Press, 2010.

Smucker, Janneken. *A New Deal for Quilts*. International Quilt Museum, University of Nebraska–Lincoln, 2023.

Taylor, P. *Telling It Like It Was: A Guide to Making Aboriginal and Torres Strait Islander History*. Canberra: Australian Institute of Aboriginal and Torres Strait Island Studies, 1996.

Terkel, Studs. *Hard Times: An Oral History of the Great Depression*. New York: Pantheon, 1970.

Valk, A., and L. Brown (eds.). *Living with Jim Crow: African American Women and Memories of the Segregated South*. New York: Palgrave Macmillan, 2010.

Zhang, X., and Sang Ye. *Chinese Lives*. New York: Pantheon, 1987.

Organizations

The International Oral History Association
The Oral History Society (United Kingdom)
The Oral History Association (United States)
Oral History Association of South Africa
Canadian Oral History
Oral History Australia
Associaçao Brasileira de História Oral
Oral History Network of Ireland
Asociación Mexicana de Historia Oral
Czech Oral History Association
FOHN—The Finnish Oral History Network
OHANZ—National Oral History Association of New Zealand (NZL)
Asociación Argentina de Historia Oral (AHORA)
China International Oral History Week (COHW), Cui Yongyuan Oral History Research Center, Communication University of China

Web Resources

OHA Principles and Best Practices, Oral History Association: https://oralhistory.org/principles-and-best-practices-revised-2018/.

OHA Principles and Best Practices, Oral History Association (Chinese): https://oralhistory.org/wp-content/uploads/2022/01/New-Chinese-OHA-Principles-and-Best-Practices.pdf.

OHA Principles and Best Practices, Oral History Association (Spanish): https://oralhistory.org/wp-content/uploads/2020/11/OHA-Best-Practices-Translation-to-Spanish-2020.pdf.

Oral History in the Digital Age: https://ohda.matrix.msu.edu.

Special Issue: "The Life Story in Oral History Practice." *Oral History* 52, no. 3 (June 2024). https://www.ohs.org.uk/wp-content/uploads/2024/08/OHJ-52-3-online.pdf.

Digital Omnium: Oral History Interviewing, Archives, and Recording Technologies: https://digitalomnium.com\.

Is Your Oral History Legal and Ethical?, Oral History Society: https://www.ohs.org.uk/legal-and-ethical-advice/.

Oral History Australia Guidelines of Ethical Practice: https://oralhistoryaustralia.org.au/guide-ethical-practice/.

Archiving Oral History: Manual of Best Practices, Oral History Association (US): https://oralhistory.org/archives-principles-and-best-practices-complete-manual.

"Remote Oral History Interviewing," Oral History Society: https://www.ohs.org.uk/covid-19-remote-recording/.

Oral History Transcription Style Guides

Style Guide: A Quick Reference for Editing Oral History Transcripts. Baylor University Institute for Oral History. https://www.baylor.edu/old/2021-02/_oralhistory/doc.php/14142.pdf.

Oral History Program Style Guide. Archives of American Art, Smithsonian Institution. https://www.aaa.si.edu/oral-history-program-style-guide-section-1-formatting.

Oral History Transcription Style Guide. Columbia University Center for Oral History. https://incite.columbia.edu/publications-old/2019/3/13/oral-history-transcription-style-guide.

Index

For the benefit of digital users, indexed terms that span two pages (e.g., 52–53) may, on occasion, appear on only one of those pages.

1964 Civil Rights March on Frankfort (Kentucky) Oral History Project 71
9/11 terrorist attacks (2001) 10, 38, 71, 94–5

A

Aboriginal oral history 8, 11–12
Accuracy of oral history 2, 19–20, 36–7
Act Up Oral History Project 5–6
Activism and social justice (documentation of) 43–4, 73–4
Africa 2–3, 5, 12–13, 20–1, 25, 30, 94–5, 106
African American oral history 2–3, 9–10, 13, 25, 29, 35–6, 60–3, 75–6, 103–4
Abernathy, Ralph 13
Academy of Motion Picture Arts and Sciences 101–2
AIDS (oral history) 5–6
Al Akhawayn University, Morocco 104–5
Alexievich, Svetlana 11
Ambedkar, B.R. 8

American Association for State and Local History (AASLH) 1
American Folklife Center, Library of Congress 5, 10. *See also* Library of Congress
American Folklore Society 19–20
American Philosophical Society 34
American University of Beirut 8, 101–2. *See also* Palestinian Oral History Archive
American University of Kuwait 101–2. *See also* Oral History and Documentation Oral History Project
An Oral History of the Electricity Supply Industry in the UK (OHESI) 79–80. *See also* National Life Stories
Anderson, Kathryn 50
Anonymity 81
Anthropologists 25–7
Anthropology 20, 25–6, 41–2
Antioch College 104–5
Apartheid 12
Aqua!Nabara oral history project (Brazil) 75

Archives 89–90, 93–110
  access 93–110
  access restrictions 80–1, 91–3
  artificial intelligence (AI) 105–6
  deeds of gift (releases) 92–3
  ethics and legal issues(archival) 93–8
  metadata 55–6, 85–6
  Oral History Metadata Synchronizer (OHMS) 100–6. *See also* OHMS
  processing 85–8, 100–4
  transcribing and transcripts 52–3, 86–8, 100–1, 105
Artificial intelligence (AI) 105–6
Asian Americans (oral history) 7–8
Australia 5, 8, 11–12, 53–4, 70–8
Australian Lives (oral history project) 5

B

Baldwin, James 13
Ballymenone, County Fermanagh, Northern Ireland 44
Bancroft, Hubert Howe 25, 34
Baum, Willa 16
Baylor University Institute for Oral History 3–4, 34, 53–4
BBC's Listening Project 36
Bede, Venerable 22
Belfast Project (Boston College) 97–8
Bellow, Saul 28–9
Benedict, Ruth 25–6
Biobaku, Saburi 21
Birmingham Civil Rights Institute Oral History Project 71
Black Women in Bourbon Oral History Project 75–6. *See also* Louie B. Nunn Center for Oral History, University of Kentucky
Bluegrass Music Hall of Fame and Museum 5–6

Bloch, Marc 35
Boas, Franz 25–7
Boder, David 29–30
Bodnar, John 36–7
Bontemps, Arna 28–9
Bornat, Joanna 14, 42
Boston College case. *See* Belfast Project (Boston College) 97–8
Boswell, James 14
Botkin, Ben 28–9
Bourbon whiskey xxi, 8, 75–6
Braudel, Fernand 35
Brazil 75
Bringing Them Home Oral History Project 8, 11–12. *See also* National Library of Australia
British Library 5, 79–81
Brokaw, Tom 10
Brooklyn Historical Society 5–6, 101–2
Bryan, Brooke Blackmon 104–5
Bryson, Anna 53–4
Bureau of American Ethnology (BAE) 25–8

C

California (oral history) 3–4, 6, 8, 15–16, 34, 50
California State University, Fullerton. *See* Center for Oral and Public History at California State University, Fullerton
California State University at Long Beach 50
Campos, Margarita (Marguerite) 28
Canada 3–4, 31–2, 39
Career Servers Oral History Project 5–6. *See also* Southern Foodways Alliance (SFA)
Carmichael, Stokely 13
Caruso, Giovanni 106–7, 109
Cave, Mark 94–5

Centre for Oral History and Digital Storytelling at Concordia University 3–4

Center for Oral and Public History, California State University, Fullerton 3–4, 34

Centre for Oral History, National and University Library of Iceland 5

Centre for Popular Memory, University of Capetown 3–4

China 3–4, 22, 84–5

Chowdhury, Indira 49

Civil rights (oral history) 8, 13, 43, 71

Coe Ridge, Kentucky 35–6

Collins, Beulah 60–3

Columbia Center for Oral History at Columbia University (CCOH) 3–4, 8, 10, 15, 17, 30–1, 34–5, 53–4

Columbia Oral History Research Office, *See* Columbia Center for Oral History at Columbia University

Community oral history 2–3, 5–6, 8, 11–13, 18–20, 35–6, 40–4, 46, 57, 73–4, 76–8, 80–1, 89

Compos, Margarita (Marguerite) 28

Copyright (of oral history interviews) 92–3

Cork Folklore Project 5–6

Covid-19 pandemic (oral history) 71, 82, 94–5

Crisis centered oral history projects 11–13, 93–5. *See also* trauma

Cramer, Jennifer A. 94–5

Creative commons licensing 93

Crossing Borders, Bridging Generations Oral History 5–6. *See also* Brooklyn Historical Society

Cui Yongyuan Center for Oral History at the Communication University of China in Beijing 3–4, 84–5

D

Dachau (concentration camp) 106, 109

Davis, Samara 76

D-Day Invasion 29, 59–60

De Berg, Hazel 70–1, 98

Deeds of gift. *See* legal releases

Defamation 71

Delhi Oralities Project, Centre of Community Knowledge (CCK) 8. *See also* University of Delhi

Defoe, Daniel 18

Denison University 104–5

Densho: The Japanese American Legacy Project 7. *See also* Densho Visual History Collection

Densho Visual History Collection 7

Densmore, Frances 27

Devine, Ralph 59–61

Dike, Kenneth Onwuka 30

Disaster (oral history), *see* crisis centered oral history projects and trauma and oral history

Documentaries and oral history 9–11, 17, 30–1, 41–2, 52–3, 74, 84–5, 102–3. *See also* Public presentation of oral history

Dorson, Richard M. 19–20

Draper, Lyman Copeland 24

E

East End Women's Museum Oral History Project (London) 71

Edison, Thomas Alva 26–7

Ellison, Ralph 28–9

England 3–5, 23, 30–2, 79–81, 89, 97, 101–2

European Union 96–7

Equipment for oral history. *See* Recording Technologies

F

Farmer, James 13
Family oral history 103–4. *See also* Genealogy
Febvre, Lucian 35
Federal Writers Project (WPA) 28–9. *See also* Works Progress Administration
Feldstein, Mark 51
Feminist oral history 35–6, 50
Fewkes, Jesse Walter 27
Filmmakers of New China Oral History Project 84–5. *See also* Cui Yongyuan Center for Oral History at the Communication University of China in Beijing
First National Colloquium on Oral History, 1966 (Lake Arrowhead) 15–16
Fletcher, Alice Cunningham 27
Folklore 18, 20, 25–9, 35–6, 41–2
Folklorists 18, 25–9
Forman Christian College, Pakistan 104–5
Formerly enslaved persons interviews 2–3, 29
Foxfire (oral history project) 9–10
Freund, Alexander 39
French Annales School (Historians) 34–5
Frisch, Michael 37, 45, 100
Fry, Gladys-Marie 35–6
Funding oral history 73–4, 87–9

G

Garbage (the band) 63–6
GDPR 96–7. *See also* General Data Protection Regulation (GDPR)
Genealogy 103. *See also* Family oral history
General Data Protection Regulation (GDPR),
Genocide oral history 6, 12–13, 94–5
German Central Historical Commission 29–30
Glassie, Henry 44
Global Liberal Arts Alliance. *See* Oral History in the Liberal Arts (OHLA)
Gluck, Sherna 35–6, 50
Goin' North: Stories from the First Great Migration to Philadelphia Oral History Project 60–3
Goin' North: Tales of the Great Migration (radio documentary) 9–10
Gould, Joseph 32–3
Grants. *See* Funding oral history
Great Lakes College Association 104–5. *See also* Oral History in the Liberal Arts (OHLA)
Grele, Ronald J. 16, 36–7
Guanabara Bay (Brazil) 75
Guidelines for Social Justice Oral History Work (Oral History Association) 73–4

H

Hall, Charles Francis 31–2
Hardy, Charles 60–3, 103–4
Harlan County, Kentucky 44–5
Harrington, John Peabody 27–8
Herodotus 22
Hesseltine, William B 1, 24
Historic New Orleans Collection 10
History (academic discipline) 20
History of the Black Movement in Brazil, Centro de Pesquisa e Documentação de História Contemporânea do Brasil (The Center for Research and Documentation of Contemporary History of Brazil) of the Getulio Vargas Foundation in Rio de Janeiro (CPDOC) 8

Hobsbawm, Eric 36-7
Hockey Museum (Surrey, England) 101-2
Holocaust (oral history) 6, 29-30
Human Subjects Research. *See* Institutional Review Boards (IRB)
Hungarian National Relief Committee for Deportees 29-30
Hurricane Katrina (oral history projects) 10, 94-5
Hurston, Zora Neale 2-3, 25-6, 28-9

I

I Remember When: Times Gone but Not Forgotten (radio documentary) 9-10
Ikeda, Tom 6
Impact of the Family Support System on Female Professionals in Pakistan (oral history project) 104-5. *See also* Forman Christian College, Pakistan
Imperial War Museum Oral History Project (UK) 71
Independent Practitioners' Toolkit for Oral Historians (Oral History Association) 73-4
India 8, 49
Indexing. *See* Archives and OHMS
Indigenous people oral history 11-12, 19-20, 23, 27, 38-9
Informed consent 55, 87, 91-2, 94, 96-7, 105. *See also* Legal releases
Institutional Review Boards (IRB) 95
International Bluegrass Music Museum (IBMM). *See* Bluegrass Music Hall of Fame and Museum
Intersubjectivity 46-9. *See also* Theory
Interviewees. *See* Narrators
Interviewers 43, 46-7, 76-8
 insiders/outsiders 77-8
 journalists and journalism 41-2, 51-3
 sharing authority 46
Interviews and Interviewing 41-69. *See also* questions
 co-creation and collaboration 46, 53, 99
 conducting 41-69
 content core 60-2, 78-9
 cropped life history 43-4
 defining component of oral history 22-34
 deep exchange 46-9, 61
 ethics 51-2, 71-4, 90-8
 ethnographic style 44-5
 follow-up questions 42-3, 56-7, 63-9
 funnel approach 66-7
 history of 22-40
 in-person vs. remote 82-3
 intentionality 14-15, 21-2, 31, 38, 42
 interview styles 42
 journalism 51-3
 Principles and Best Practices (OHA) 52, 73-4
 qualitative interviewing 42
 research 54
Ireland 5-6, 19, 97
Irish oral history 44, 97-8
Italy 106-9

J

JWells 76
Jack, Dana C. 50
Japan 8
Jewish Historical Institute 29-30
Johnson, Samuel 14

Jordan, Vernon 13
Journalism and journalists 41–2, 51–3

K

Keio University 8
Kelly, Arthur 59–60, 109
Kentucky Historical Society 58–9
Kentucky (oral history) 24, 35–6, 44, 106–9
Kentucky Oral History Commission 89
Kennedy, Stetson 28–9
King, Martin Luther, Jr. 13
Kossola, Oluale 2–3. *See also* Cudjo Lewis
Krauss, Taylor 12–13
Kroeber, A. L. 25–6

L

Legal releases 92–3. *See also* archives
Lewis, Cudjo 2–3. *See also* Oluale Kossola
Llewellyn, Kristina R. 35–9
LGBTQ+ oral history projects 8, 81
Libraries and oral history 5–6, 101–2
Library of Congress 5, 28–9
Life history approach 43, 71
Lomax, John 29
Los Angeles Psychoanalytical Society 34
Louie B. Nunn Center for Oral History, University of Kentucky xx–xxi, 3–4, 8, 34, 75–6, 100–1, 103–4. *See also* University of Kentucky
Lowie, Robert 19–20
Lynd, Alice 35
Lynd, Staughton 35

M

Mahuika, Nepia 38
McClain, Gillian 9–10
McConville, Sean 53–4
McNeil, Leggs 9–10
Majdanek (concentration camp) 29–30
Manson, Shirley 63–6
Mead, Margaret 25–6
Memory 21, 24, 35–6, 40, 47, 62, 75
 collective 19–20
 nostalgia 37
 reliability of 1, 20, 36–7
Memories of Brazilians Project (Projeto Memórias dos Brasileiros) 5–6
Mexico 23
Michelet, Jules 23
Microphones 83–5, 88
Military oral history projects 10, 29, 59–61, 67–9, 71, 106–9
Mississippi Freedom Project (oral history project) 8. *See also* Samuel Proctor Oral History Program at the University of Florida
Mitchell, Joseph 32–3
Montell, Lynwood 35–6
Morrissey, Charles T. 14–15, 31, 63
Museo da Pessoa in Brazil 5–6
Museums and oral history 5–6, 10–11, 17, 39, 71, 74–5, 101–2

N

Narrators 43–7, 79–80
Narrator review (transcripts) 87
National Archive of the Dominican Republic (Archivo General de la Nación) 5
National Archives of Singapore 5, 16–17, 53–4

National Archives of the United Arab Emirates Ministry of Presidential Affairs 5
National Film Video and Sound Archives (a component of the National Archives and Records Service of South Africa) 5
National Library of Australia 5, 8, 11–12, 70–1
National Library of New Zealand (Te Puna Mātauranga o Aotearoa) 5
National Life Stories 5, 79–80
National Lottery Heritage Fund (UK) 89
National Park Service 8, 10
National Public Radio (NPR) 9–10
Native Americans (oral history) 19–20, 25–7
  Chinook 25–6
  Chumash 27
  Guna 28
  Inuit 31–2
  Kiowa 27
  Kitanemuk 27
  Kwakiutl 25–6
  Mojave 27
  Navajo xxi
  Passamaquoddy 27
  Serrano 27
  Tsimshian 25–6
  Yuma 27
Nebraska State Historical Society 34
Neuenschwander, John A. 91, 93,
Nevins, Allan 15, 17, 30, 32–5
NHS at 70: The Story of Our Lives, Centre for the History of Science, Technology and Medicine 8
Nigeria 21, 30
Norris Logan, Deborah 23–4
Northern Ireland 44, 97–8
Nostalgia 37, 51. *See also* Memory

Nottingham–Trent University 89. *See also* The Hidden Heritage of Wellbeing in the Community: Co Creating Oral Histories of Mental Health Care (oral history project)

O

Oberlin University 104–5
OHA. *See* Oral History Association (USA)
OHMS, (Oral History Metadata Synchronizer) 100–6. *See also* archives
Oklahoma State University Oral History Research Program 3–4
Oral history
  as a field and practice 41–2
  as oral tradition 17–20, 30
  best practices 53–4, 72–4
  collaborative nature 53, 80–1, 90–1, 95, 104–5
  criticisms of 1–2, 36–7
  defining 2, 14–17, 36, 38–40
  functions of 11–13
  international differences in approach 36, 39–40
  interviews and interviewing 41–69
  journalism 41–2, 51–3
  labor history 35
  meaning 3, 36–7, 47–8, 50, 52, 66–9
  multidisciplinary nature of 20, 30–1, 41–2
  project design 70–98
  project funding 87–9
  project partnerships 89–90
  reliability and accuracy of 2, 19–20, 36–7
  role in healing 11–12
  selecting narrators 79–80
  shared authority 45–6, 53

Oral history (*Continued*)
teaching. *See* Pedagogy and oral history
training 4, 12, 53-4, 76-8
trauma-informed 11-13
Oral History and Cultural Heritage of Morrocco Oral History Project 104-5. *See also* Al Akhawayn University, Morrocco
Oral History and Documentation Oral History Project 101-2. *See also* American University of Kuwait
Oral History Association (Australia). *See* Oral History Australia
Oral History Association (USA) xxi, 15-16, 34, 52-4, 73-4, 90-1
Oral History Australia 53-4
Oral History Center, University of California Berkeley 3-4, 8, 34
Oral History in the Liberal Arts (OHLA) 104-5
Oral History Metadata Synchronizer (OHMS). *See* OHMS (Oral History Metadata Synchronizer)
Oral History Network of Ireland 97
Oral History of Prostitution (oral history project) 80-1
Oral History Program of the University of Buenos Aires (Programa de Historia Oral de la Universidad de Buenos Aires) 3-4
Oral history projects 5-8, 38, 43, 45, 71
Oral History Society (UK) 36, 53-4
Oral History Unit and Collective at Newcastle University 3-4
Oral tradition 17-22, 30

P

Pacific Standard Time: LA/LA Oral History Project 101-2. *See also* Academy of Motion Picture Arts and Sciences
Palestinian Oral History Archive 8, 101-2. *See also* American University of Beirut
Parsons, Elsie Clews 27
Passerini, Luisa 37
Pearson, Tanya 63-6
Pedagogy and oral history 41-2, 103-5
Philadelphia, Pennsylvania 23, 25, 32, 34, 60-2
Plimpton, George 9-10
Pogue, Forrest C. 29
Poland 29-30
Portelli, Alessandro 36-7, 44-8
Pramanik, Dipali 49
Principles and Best Practices (Oral History Association) 52, 73-4
Privacy and oral history 91, 96-7, 105
Project design 70-98
content core 78-9
controversial or high-risk topics 80-1
interviewers 76-8
project blueprint 72, 109-10
project mission statement 74-6
recording technologies 82-5. *See also* recording technologies
selecting narrators 79-80
Public presentation of oral history
archives and libraries 10-11, 93-110
documentaries 9-11, 17, 30-1, 41-2, 52-3, 74, 84-5, 102-3
museum exhibits 5-6, 10-11, 74, 103-4
podcasts and podcasting 10-11, 52-3, 74
radio 9-11, 17
Publishing oral history 9-10

Q

Queer Newark Oral History, Rutgers University—Newark 8
Questions 55–69
  follow-up 42–3, 56–7, 63–9
  leading 58–9
  open ended 45, 56

R

Radin, Paul 27
Radio and oral history. *See* Public presentation of oral history
Ranke, Leopld von 20–1
Recording technologies 2–3, 10, 17, 26–7, 29–30, 34, 82–5, 99–100
  audio recording 2–3, 10, 82–5, 88, 94, 99–100
  microphones xx–lxxii, 84–5, 88
  remote interviewing 82
  video recording 2–3, 5–6, 10, 12–13, 74–5, 82–5, 88–90, 99–100
Regional Memory and Image Before the Great East Japan Earthquake Oral History Project 8
Regional Oral History Office (ROHO). *See* Oral History Center, University of California Berkeley
Reilly, Nolan 39
Rickard, Wendy 80–1
Ritchie, Donald A. 17, 53–4, 99–100
Roberts, Helen Heffrom 27
Robertson, Beth M. 53–4
Rosie the Riveter WWII American Homefront Oral History Project 8. *See also* Oral History Center, University of California Berkeley and National Park Service
Rule of Law Oral History Project 8. *See also* Columbia Center for Oral History
Rwanda 12, 94–5

S

Sahagún, Bernardino de 23
Sahlins, Marshall 20–1
Samuel Proctor Oral History Program at the University of Florida 3–4, 8
Sapir, Edward 25–6
Shane, John Dabney 24
Shared authority 45–6, 53, 95
Sharpless, Rebecca 36–7
Shoah Foundation 6. *See also* University of Southern California (USC) Shoah Foundation
Shopes, Linda 14–15
Slave Narratives from the Federal Writers' Project 29. *See also* Formerly enslaved persons interviews
Slavery 2–3, 29. *See also* Formerly enslaved persons interviews
Smithsonian Institution 25–6
Smucker, Janneken 103–4
South Africa (oral history) 5, 12, 25
South African Democracy Education Trust (SADET) Oral History Project 12
South African History Project (SAHP) 12
Southern Foodways Alliance (SFA) 5–6
Southern Oral History Program 3–4. *See also* University of North Carolina at Chapel Hill
Special Collections Research Center, University of Kentucky Libraries 107–9

Spielberg, Steven 6
Starr, Louie 33
Stein, Jean 9–10
Still, William 25
StoryCorps 36
Stuart, James 25

T

T. Harry Williams Center for Oral History, Louisiana State University 10, 94–5
Tanagi Aburano, Sharon 7
Teaching oral history. *See* Pedagogy and oral history
Terkel, Studs 9–10, 28–9
The Hidden Heritage of Wellbeing in the Community: Co Creating Oral Histories of Mental Health Care (oral history project) 89. *See also* Nottingham-Trent University
Theory
  memory 21, 24, 35–6, 40, 47, 62, 75
  intersubjectivity 46–9
  shared authority 45–6, 53
Thomson, Allistair 36–7, 39–40
Thompson, E. P. 35
Thompson, Paul 2, 14, 36–7, 42
Thucydides 22
TikTok 83–4
Tonkin, Elizabeth 36–7
Transcription 52–3, 86–8, 100–1, 105
Trauma and oral history 93–5
Tremensuoli, Minturno, Italy 106–9
Trevor-Roper, Hugh 20–1
Truth and Reconciliation Commission, South Africa 12
Tuchman, Barbara 36–7

U

United Kingdom 36, 53–4, 71, 80–1, 89, 96–7
University of Buenos Aires 3–4
University of California at Berkeley. *See* Oral History Center, University of California Berkeley
University of California–Los Angeles (UCLA) 34
University of Delhi 8
University of Georgia 101–2
University of Kentucky. *See* Louie B. Nunn Center for Oral History, University of Kentucky
University of Manchester 8
University of North Carolina at Chapel Hill 3–4. *See also* Southern Oral History Program
University of North Texas 34
University of Southern California (USC) Shoah Foundation 6. *See also* Shoah Foundation
University of Southern Mississippi 10
University of Texas at Austin. *See* Voces Oral History Project
University of Tsukaba 8
University of Wisconsin–Madison Oral History Program 3–4, 101–2
Urca Institute, Rio de Janeiro, Brazil 75

V

Vansina, Jan 21
Vermont Historical Society 31
Veterans History Project 5, 10. *See also* American Folklife Center, Library of Congress
Video oral history. *See* recording technologies
Voces Oral History Project, University of Texas at Austin 8, 84–5
Voices of Rwanda Archive 12–13
Voice of Witness 12–13
Voltaire 23

W

Warren, Robert Penn 13
Watson, John Fanning 23
Watson, Winslow Cossoul 31
Webb, Marshall A. 106–10
Webb, Opal 107–9
Webb, Roger 107–9
West Bengal, India 49
West Chester University 103–4
White, Sir Harold 70–1
Wigginton, Eliot 9–10
Women in Bourbon Oral History Project, Louie B. Nunn Center for Oral History, University of Kentucky Libraries 8, 75
Women of Rock Oral History Project 63–6. *See also* Pearson, Tanya.
Women's oral history 8, 35–6, 50, 63–6, 70–1, 75–6
Working Lives (radio documentary) 9–10
World War II 29, 106–9
Works Progress Administration (WPA) 28–9. *See also* Federal Writers Project (WPA)
Wright, Richard 28–9

X

X, Malcolm 13

Y

Yezierska, Anzia 28–9
YouTube 83–4
Young, Andrew 13
Young, Whitney 13
Yiddish Book Center's Wexler Oral History Project 75, 84–5, 101–2

Z

Zahn, Steve 67–9, 102
Zulu (oral history) 25

WRITING AND SCRIPT
A Very Short Introduction
Andrew Robinson

Without writing, there would be no records, no history, no books, and no emails. Writing is an integral and essential part of our lives; but when did it start? Why do we all write differently and how did writing develop into what we use today? All of these questions are answered in this *Very Short Introduction*. Starting with the origins of writing five thousand years ago, with cuneiform and Egyptian hieroglyphs, Andrew Robinson explains how these early forms of writing developed into hundreds of scripts including the Roman alphabet and the Chinese characters.

'User-friendly survey.'

Steven Poole, The Guardian

www.oup.com/vsi